D1571051

ALBUMS OF EARLY LIFE

ALBUMS OF EARLY LIFE

STANLEY KAUFFMANN

New Haven and New York

Ticknor & Fields

1980

These Albums have appeared previously in: *American Poetry Review, American Review, The American Scholar, Bennington Review, Cosmopolitan, Harper's Magazine,* and *The Hudson Review.*

Library of Congress Cataloging in Publication Data

Kauffmann, Stanley, 1916–
  Albums of early life.

  1. Kauffmann, Stanley, 1916–   —Biography.
2. Authors, American — 20th century — Biography.
3. Critics — United States — Biography. I. Title.
PS3521.A7255Z462   818'.5203 [B]   80-14481
ISBN 0-89919-015-4

00 10 9 8 7 6 5 4 3 2 1

Printed in the United States of America

Many names of persons and places have been changed.

Thanks to the John Simon Guggenheim Memorial Foundation for a fellowship and to the Rockefeller Foundation for a sojourn at the Villa Serbelloni in Bellagio, both of which awards helped in this work.

To Laura

Some time after these Albums were begun, I saw Fellini's *Amarcord*. A few words from my review may serve as epigraph here:

> For everyone, the figures of the past, pleasant and unpleasant, become rarefied through the years into talismans. . . . Memory is the only place toward which life heads certainly.

CONTENTS

ONE

Album of Farms   3
Album of My Mother   21
Album of Older Women   29

TWO

Album of a Director   45
Album of Comic-Book Life   103
Album of a Volunteer Orderly   125
Album of a Play Doctor   141

THREE

Album of Suicides   165
Album of London, 1951   197
Album of a Western Writer   219

ONE

Album of Farms

1

DROWNING. The first drowning when I was four. A swimming hole in the country, where we were boarding. A grassy bank with sun. Mothers in clusters. Children in yelling files, leaping and waving into the water. I remember hearing that there was a whirlpool at one edge of the hole and being told not to go near. I don't remember going near, but suddenly I was in it.

Above me a twisting funnel of water, with light at the far large end. My lungs weeping and choking. Up once and a smash of sound, then down again into the funnel and up again with my mouth open. The water flowed through me. I felt I was joining the water, I wouldn't drown, I would flow away, and I was more fascinated than scared. How would it happen? Then my hair was pulled upward.

I remember the body of the young man who pulled me out, lean and brown, but not his face. My mother enfolded me. My quick recovery. Later that afternoon I was running around. But on the other side of the green bank and my mother's arms and the brown strong swimmer is the funnel above me, with the light at the end and the sense of being a spectator while I died. It recurs — fateful but not frightening — in my dreams and in my day-dreams, in my life.

2

Farms. It was the word of wonder. Others, in the backs of their brains, have sea and sand, blue and white. For me, it is green and brown and hay-gold sloping up steep hills, the smell of hay and of flanks, cows and horses. Perhaps it was because of the swimming hole that I never wanted the sea. We went to farms, and farmers didn't swim, they had no time. Besides, these farms were in mountains, where there were only brooks.

But it was not flight in my mind, it was desire. The city was bare and dirty and very small in its life, no matter how big. City men could do nothing. The country was everything else. Farms were what the country was for. Farmers could do everything.

The other boarders at these farms, and their children, they were the city, too. I avoided them. I stayed with the farmers. I trailed them. They teased, but they were amused, and they taught me when I tried their jobs. I learned, and they were pleased. I ate with them in the kitchen instead of the boarders' dining room, and I learned to eat like them, my left arm around the plate and my right arm shoveling. I worked with them as much as they would allow. By the time I was six, I could milk, I knew all about harness even if I couldn't lift it all, I could drive a team if there was no trouble, I could almost drive a hay-rake, I could tromp down the hay on a wagon or in a mow. By the time I was eight, a farmer asked my mother whether I could come work for him the summer I was nine. He wouldn't pay, but she could come and visit for two weeks board free. She knew them and knew I would eat well and sleep quilted.

It happened every summer then, for six years until I went to college, that I was not a boarder. For two months and a bit, I was part of the country. One day a car stopped on our dirt road, and the city man driving saw me in overalls and high shoes laced over the ankles and said, "Hey, son, how do I get to Kimball's place?" I told him in flawless country accent. I was happy.

When I was twelve, I went to another farm nearby, a big one for those parts, with two teams. Walt ran the place for the woman who owned it. He was burly and sandy and had a cast in his eye, and he teased me and bossed me. He gave me one of the teams for the summer, to be my charge and to work with. They were black mares, not young but strong: Queenie and Bess. Bess was blind with cataracts but could work perfectly with the other mare. I cleaned them and their stalls and harnessed and worked them and cooled them and watered and fed them. When I made a mistake, Walt said, "Call yourself a teamster?" Teamster! I never wanted to leave.

One day I was harnessing Queenie when she was in heat. I had been told that they were skittish then, but when I reached under her for the bellyband, I rubbed her sensitive skin. Like fire, she kicked upward with a hind leg. She kicked my hand into her belly. If it had been into anything hard, the hand would have been broken. I remember my hand being kicked into that softness, I remember the sting but also the warmth. I felt strong and familiar and said, "*So* now, you bitch. Here! *So* there, damn you," and felt my hand ache and kept on working.

3

Johnny Mac the Scotchman was the farmer I left to go to Walt's. One night Walt's barn floor had collapsed, and Johnny had gone over, along with other neighbors, to help out. He had taken me along. Walt saw me work, pitching out hay by lamplight, and asked whether I'd like to come over there next summer. Walt's place was larger, and I would have my own team. Besides, Johnny and his wife fought a lot. So I went. Johnny and I were still friendly when we met, but there was a proud tone in him as if he forgave me for wanting to better myself.

One morning in the middle of my first summer at Walt's there was a phone call for Nellie, who owned the place. Afterward, she called Walt over, and I could see them murmuring together. Then Walt told me, as if it were a favor, the way he always told me adult news, that Johnny Mac had been found dead in his milkhouse. He was epileptic, which I had never known, had fallen into the milk vat in the middle of a fit, and had drowned.

For three summers I had always been with Johnny at milking time. It had nothing to do with me, this death, it could have happened spring or fall or winter, even if I had never left him, I wouldn't have been around then anyway; but secretly I took it as my fault. If I hadn't left him, he would still be alive! I knew even then it was flimsy, I was pretending, but it was my first chance to have a quiet sorrow, a guilt that was worth not talking about.

4

Fetching the cows was boy's work. That was one reason they hired me. These were dairy farms, and during the busy haying season, a man wouldn't have to leave the fields early to go for the cows at milking time. But I also fetched them for the morning milking. I asked to do that. Walt thought I was silly and said, "Sure."

I was up at four-thirty and climbed the hill of the night pasture at quarter to five. It was still quite dark and, rain or no rain, very wet. I would cross the stone wall and trudge up the slope listening to the sound of my boots in the wet grass, listening for the tinkle of the one belled cow above me.

The light would be coming by the time I got up there. As I approached, I could hear the cows grazing. Only a few would be sleeping or even lying down. They would turn their heads and look at me easily, as if they understood that only someone who really had something to do with them would be up on the mountain with them at that hour.

I called to them. "Co', boss. Co', bossy." I moved around the outside and started them down. I counted in the coming light. Thirty-one. As we descended, they moved ahead of me in clumping grace, making me feel great and attended. When one stopped and arched her back, I knew it was to piss. They could shit while they walked. I liked them to do both.

Now as we came lower, the sun appeared behind the

mountains to the east. The ridges were glistening while the valley was still black. The windows would light up in the house below, Nellie and her mother in the kitchen to finish all the day's baking before breakfast. The one bell tinkled. The hooves plodded stately in the damp. The mist below shredded and rose into the sun. The smell was of everything beginning.

Afternoons were different, especially on sticky August days. One hot afternoon when I got to the top of the day pasture, I couldn't make the cows move. I called, I threw stones, the ones I chased would budge a little, and as soon as I went after the others, the first ones would stop. The heat made them mean, and the flies tormented them. A couple of them raised their tails like banners and ran through the woods to chase the flies off. Others slopped into the swamp where it was hard for me to chase them and head them. I couldn't believe that these were the same creatures with whom I had come down through the dawn that very day.

Nothing worked. They balked and stood. After a while my throat got tight, and I retreated from my new maturity to rely on the boyhood to which I still had some claim. I broke and ran all the way down to the barn, almost in tears, to where Walt was driving a team on the hayfork. I told him I simply couldn't move the cows, they wouldn't heed. I expected him to recognize the remnants of boy in me, tease a little, and take over.

His mouth thinned out, "You get your ass back up that hill," he said confidentially, "or I'll boot it off this place." I was shocked. I had not resorted to boyhood for some time, but I had thought it would still work. I don't think I ever used it again.

I went all the way up the hill again, the best part of a

mile. This time I got the cows started. I knew there was no choice. It wasn't fear of Walt himself or any lesson in grit. I didn't want to be fired. I didn't want to lose the cows, their other selves, the morning creatures they had been and would be again. Their afternoon selves didn't matter. I could endure them, in between the mornings.

5

A circus had pitched its tents on Tyler's Flats, alongside the state road just the other side of Hubbell Corners. I walked down after supper one night. I met some boys I knew, and we looked at the side shows before the circus began.

As we moved to the ticket booth, a fat man with a broad-brimmed hat and a hoarse split voice asked us whether we would like to get in free. All we had to do was wait after the show was over and help load the benches on the trucks. I had money in my pocket, but I wanted to do it, to have the story to tell when I got back to the city in the fall. I said yes, and so did the others. The fat man asked for our belts as security, so that we wouldn't scoot after the show.

The circus was tatty but cozy. Afterward, the man gave us back our belts and we loaded benches onto a couple of trucks. It took only about half an hour, but before we finished, everyone who might have given me a lift back up to the farm had left.

I walked home alone. It was completely dark. I have never again been, outdoors, in such dark. No stars, no

9

hint of difference even to make trees seem blacker than the sky. It was about a mile and a half up the dirt road to the farm, and I walked uphill through this black lake. I knew the road well. I had walked it many times in summer and snow, had driven horses over it often. I could tell where I was by the cant of the road, almost by the ruts. When I came to a turn or a rise, I could see it in my mind, and I knew how far before the next turn. But I saw absolutely nothing.

I felt comfortable and fine. To know some part of the earth so well that it belonged to me in the dark. I felt easy and free. I walked up the mountain alone and felt that everything around me was mine.

The only other time I had that feeling was almost thirty years later in Rome. One Sunday morning in December I had to get up early to take a train. At six o'clock I left the small hotel, walked over to the Via Condotti and up to the Piazza di Spagna to find a taxi. I was absolutely alone. Not another person, not a car, not a dog. Nothing. It was clear, gold morning, and the ancient city belonged to me.

The light was like joy, but it reminded me of that complete dark. Both times, sunlight and black, I seemed to hear for miles and miles, and heard silence. Everything was mine.

6

Orrie Nichols, the hired man, had only three fingers on his left hand. A childhood mishap with a mowing machine. He was about forty, had pop-eyes of blue, something close to a cleft palate, and he worked hard. His maimed hand made no difference. When he set about some job, like cocking up the windrows in a field that had just been raked, he worked more intensely than anyone could have paid him for. At thirteen, working alongside him, I could see the difference in our universes. His was complete, and he occupied it completely.

Saturday nights he dressed to go out, with his mail-order suit, clip-on bow, turned-up brim, and long curved pipe with a tiny bowl. He looked as if some college boy had dressed him as a mock college boy. Often he would come home drunk, late at night, breathe heavily and bump a little as he climbed the stairs and went past my door. The rest of the time he just worked. We worked and ate together. He was not withdrawn or morose, he laughed a lot with a whinny, still we never talked much, except about work.

One Sunday there was an airplane down at Tyler's Flats, where the circus had played. The *Roxbury Times* had announced that it was coming, that you could go up for ten minutes for five dollars. Orrie, who never went anywhere except to fairs and to places where he could get home-brew, had torn out the announcement. That Sunday he said he was walking down to the Flats, and he invited me to go with him. He was wearing his college clothes. I put on some clean clothes, and we went.

We stood at the side of Tyler's Flats with a crowd of others and watched the little monoplane take off and land in ten-minute flights. Two passengers at a time. Orrie had got excited when he first saw the plane, and the longer we watched, the higher-pitched his voice became, the more he laughed his whinny. After about an hour or so, he said to me, "B'God, let's give her a try. I'll treat you, b'God." Ten dollars was a lot of money to Orrie.

I was grateful and impressed by the offer. Like him, I

11

had never been in a plane before. I was a little scared. I knew my parents would be upset if they found out, even if nothing happened. But I had no choice, and I was glad of it.

Orrie paid the pilot for both of us, and we climbed in behind him. The plane bumped across the field. Orrie whinnied softly a few times as we started, but after we took off, he was quiet. I gripped the edges of the seat and was surprised to find that I wasn't frightened or sick. I was more surprised to find that I couldn't recognize anything below. The pilot had headed north, we must have flown over our farm, but I wasn't sure I recognized the house.

I looked at Orrie. His face was serious as he looked out, as if he were listening. His mouth gaped a little, but his brows were knotted as when he was untangling harness. His three-fingered hand gripped the window ledge tightly.

We bumped down and rolled across the field. Orrie whinnied again. When the motor stopped, the pilot tore two coupons from a book for us. They certified that we had been up in an airplane, and they bore the facsimile signature of Casey Jones, a famous pilot of the time, who ran a company that had a fleet of barnstorming planes.

I thanked Orrie, and we walked home. It was hard to believe that this was the same ground that had just looked so different.

Nellie said, "My land," when we told her. Walt made some teasing remark, plainly jealous.

Orrie still didn't talk much to me from then on. The plane ride hadn't made any special bond between us. There was no change at all in him that I could see. The change was in me, about him. On Saturday nights, when he bumped drunk along the hall, I thought of his face in the plane, listening, the three-fingered hand clutching the view.

7

I had the blood lust of a boy. On Christmas vacation, when I was up visiting the farm, I asked to be the one to stick the knife in the hog's throat when they were butchering it. They agreed because they needed me. There were two men on the farm, Walt and Orrie, and two neighbors. It took four men to catch the hog, to turn it on its back and hold it there, each man hanging on to a leg. Then I took a knife, slimmed to a stiletto by years of sharpening, and as Walt directed, I felt along the underthroat for the hard spot, then for the soft spot just below it. I slit the skin gently. Then, with my left hand, I poised the knife in the slit and rammed it in with my right palm. I turned it, sunk to the hilt, round and round. I loved it. Then I pulled it out and we all ran for the fence. The hog got up quickly, furious, charged about the pigpen leaking sloshes of blood all over the mud, grew tipsy, then wildly drunk, then fell on its side, twitched, shit, and died. The men hung it up in the barn by the hind legs to dress it, and I helped scoop out the yards and yards of slippery red and yellow tubing.

So the following summer when Walt's old dog had to be killed, I volunteered. Trixie was lame, smelly, and useless, but what settled it was that she could no longer eat. Her teeth were almost gone, her gums were sore, she just moped and stank and could hardly walk. Walt said he couldn't do it himself. He had raised her from a pup, she had licked milk from his fingers. When he had been out late, she had waited for him by the road in any weather. Tears welled in his crossed eyes. He couldn't do it, but it had to be done. I said that if he wanted, I would do it for him.

He gave me an old can of chloroform that was left over from some earlier dispatch, and I took it, a rag, and Trixie into the cow barn. I slid the big door shut. She and I were alone. She was too tired to be suspicious, and she sat still when I approached. I doused the rag as Walt had instructed and held it over her patient muzzle for minutes. Nothing happened. She blinked at me. I took the rag away. She whimpered and licked my hand. I doused the rag again and smothered her again for minutes. Again she just blinked and lay there, stinking and breathing. I went out and reported to Walt, who was sitting under a tree, pale. He sniffed the can and said he guessed the stuff had got weak. He was gentle with me, which wasn't usual when I bumbled a job. He went into the cow barn and brought Trixie out and patted her. Then he and I went off to some other chore.

A few nights later after supper, I suddenly noticed that Walt was not sitting around with us in the kitchen. Trixie was gone. Just about the time I noticed this, I heard a shot. I looked at the others in the room. They were not surprised. I knew at once that I was not supposed to say anything about it or go outside. Some time later, in the gloom, I saw Walt coming back across the lower pasture toward the barn carrying his shotgun and a spade. He looked immense in the faint light.

Ten or twelve years later, one of the neighbors stopped by to see me on a trip to New York for a ball game. We took out some past experiences, like photographs, and looked at them together. Then I asked about Walt. He told me that one night a few years before, Walt had gone down below the barn with his shotgun and blown his head off. He had some incurable disease.

I suddenly saw him crossing the pasture, this time smaller.

8

Joe Moore was a tall and grave and catarrhal farmer, with a voice that sounded of the pipe that was usually in his mouth. He hawked and spit, and puffed at his little pipe, and seemed to me a very complete organism, with work clothes molded to his body. I heard rumors of his money troubles and a bad check, which made him more mature and mysterious to me. They also said he was having trouble with his daughter Sarah, who was three years older than I and wouldn't even look at me. She was said to be wild. I had seen chuckling at the filling station that came to a quick stop when Joe approached.

One day when Walt and I were in the general store, Joe came in. He and Walt exchanged greetings, and Joe bobbed his pipe at me. They talked of calves and milk prices and weather, then Joe said he was going up the mountain past our place the next day to do some berrying. I heard myself say, "Can I go with you?" I loved to pick blackberries, but I was surprised at my nerve.

Joe looked at me more serious than surprised.

I said, "Walt, you said the swale would take another day to dry out. Tomorrow'd be a good day to go." Walt admitted it reluctantly, as if he didn't want to force Joe.

Joe said, "This is real berrying, boy. Not like when the women do it. I mean to pick. Think you can keep up the whole day?"

I knew I could, and I said so.

At supper that night Walt made fun of me to the others, teasing me about getting tired with Joe and crying for my mother. Then he and the others exchanged some soft comments, that Joe might better be doing other things than pick berries, considering the state of his affairs and his family.

Next morning after breakfast, Joe arrived in his pickup truck. He had two milk pails, a butter pail, and his lunch. I had one milk pail, a butter pail, and my lunch. He bobbed his pipe once at me, waved at Walt in the barn doorway, and we drove up to the end of the road, to the abandoned farm. We didn't speak much. I thought that starting a conversation would seem boyish, and he had nothing to say. We left the truck and walked up the broad steep slope of the mountain meadow, all clover and mint and thyme, to the blanket of woods at the top. I knew there were berries, I had been there before.

In the woods we came to the glades where the bushes were thick. The light came down through the trees as through high windows. The place was still and scented with heartbreak.

We set down our milk pails and our lunches, we hung the butter pails from our belts. Then we began. The bushes were heavy with berries in middle August. There had been rain two days ago, which was why I had the day off, and then the sun had ripened them all. They gleamed and smelled. I rolled down my sleeves against the briers and went in. I liked the briers. I even liked being stuck with them once in a while, but I liked conquering them, taking a branch carefully and twisting it aside around another branch, then moving forward like a burglar amid alarms.

I knew not to budge until I had picked every berry in sight, lest I knock off some ripe ones. I knew to bend and look upward before I moved because there were always some hidden under leaves. I knew never to eat one while picking.

I dropped the berries into the pail at my waist, and the pink-pank on the tin bottom ceased as it was covered, and the perfume came up. When the pail was almost full, I went and emptied it into the milk pail. The first time I went out, Joe had already emptied some into his milk pail. I could see his cap, off there in the bushes.

Around noon when I came back for the third or fourth time to empty my pail, Joe was sitting under a tree. His first milk pail was almost full, mine about two-thirds. He nodded and said, "Good worker. 'Bout time for dinner, hain't it?"

I got my lunch and sat against a tree near him, feeling stronger than when we had started. He put his pipe on a stone and opened his paper bag. He asked me a question, about where I lived in the city. The fact that he asked me anything was startling. I answered, and we talked. He asked how many summers I'd been working on farms. We talked about his summers when he was my age. We talked about baseball. His face seemed to lighten. We talked about the Roxbury team. He hadn't had the chance to see a game that year, but he knew most of the players.

After lunch he said, "Say, I b'lieve I know." He led me through the woods to a big mossy rock. Under it a spring bubbled. "Jes' what we need," he said. He threw himself prone, took off his cap, and drank. Then he brushed the surface of the water for me, and I lay down and drank.

That afternoon he stayed near me as we picked, so we

could keep on talking. He told me about where he had grown up and gone to school, over the mountain in the next county, about some of his fights in the schoolyard and behind the woodshed.

By midafternoon, when we came out to empty our butter pails at the same time, my milk pail was full and he was well into his second. "Hell, that's enough," he said. "Let's quit early and not tell nobody. Anyway, I got an idee."

We stowed our berries down in the truck. Then he led me through the sun, past the abandoned farmhouse, to a small brook. In one place there was a pool just big enough to lie down in and get covered, with smooth washed stones on the bottom. "We might's well," he said. He tried to keep his face grave, but he grinned a little. We took off our clothes, and I saw again how white a farmer's body is compared to his face and neck and hands and forearms. We took turns lying in the icy pool, shivering and laughing. Then we came out and lay on the grass in the sun, drying and talking.

By and by he got up, naked, took a jackknife from his pants pocket and walked over to some bushes. He cut a branch. "Here's somethin' I bet you never see," he said. I asked him what it was. "Whistle wood."

He trimmed off a length about eight inches. It was hollow. Then he cut a notch in it near one end, like the notch in a whistle. Then he blew in the end, and it whistled.

He lay down again next to me and tootled on it. I laughed and said it was great.

"Yep," he said, "I knew them as could put holes along of the top and play regular tunes on it." He handed it to me. "You want it?"

I thanked him. I tried a few notes myself, and we laughed. Soon we heard a cowbell tinkling far across the valley. Some farmer was driving his cows in for milking.

Joe reached for his pants and pulled out the watch that hung from his belt by a leather thong. His face changed.

"Time to go," he said.

9

All through the New York winter I got the summer every week. The *Roxbury Times* was a poor sheet, stuffed with syndicated fillers and badly printed, but it came weekly into the stone city from the green heaven, and the news notes were full of the names that were godlike to me, the ads were of stores that I thought wonderfuly old. One week there was a news note that Carol Becker had pneumonia and had been taken to the Oneonta hospital.

She and I had kissed the summer before. She was a chunky girl of fifteen, a year older than I, who swam often in the pool I had helped to make by damming the creek with logs and stones. While she and the others dove and swam, I dabbled and floated on a raft. After the whirlpool, I had never learned to swim.

Carol was friendly but meaty and attracted me less than the other girls, some of whom were less friendly. I never thought of asking her for a date.

One night after supper, Duncan, the sixteen-year-old son of a nearby farmer, asked me to go for a ride. He wasn't going any place in particular, just his young nuts driving him crazy. I jumped at the invitation, and we wound down the hill in his father's new Chevrolet. When we got to the state road, he turned left, and soon we saw two girls sitting on the bridge railing. One was Carol, the other was prettier.

Dunc stopped and asked them to go for a ride with us. They giggled and teased for a few moments, but they knew we knew that they were sitting there in the hope that some boys would come along. Soon they simpered and shrugged and got in. Dunc drove up to the creamery and parked in the shed behind. He got in the back of the car with the other girl. Carol moved into the front with me, mostly because she wasn't wanted in the back. We kissed as if it were our duty but not too bad. A bout of kissing, then a rest, then another bout, while Duncan and his girl were rustling in the dark back seat for a couple of hours.

After I was back in New York that fall, I got a letter from Carol. It began "Dear Swiming Pal" and went on to tell me things that she and our friends had been doing since I left. She had very little charm even in her letter, but I liked the earnest way she had written the misspelled word.

When I read about her pneumonia the following winter, I remembered her little mouth pressing mine tightly and yet rather cool. The next week I read in the Roxbury paper that she had died. She was the first person I knew, of my own age or near it, to die.

I was awestruck. A girl I had actually kissed had achieved that mysterious state. It made me feel linked with large mysteries. Lips that I had kissed were now in a coffin, in a grave. It made me feel experienced and important.

But it seemed odd that this girl, nice but so unexceptional, had been chosen for this honor. A girl who didn't even know how to spell "swimming" already knew the answers to the biggest questions. There was something silly about it.

Album of My Mother

1

THERE ARE TWO. One is the woman I watched grow old
before she was old, and broken. The other is the child in
the photograph, who never changes.

She is nine. She is in the new white dress that her
mother made, with high ruffs on the shoulders and a big
bow at the waist. She has white stockings and soft white
slippers with buttoned straps. Her feet are on a cushion
and her ankles are crossed. She sits on a wicker bench
over which her skirt is spread carefully.

Her hands lie in her lap. In one hand she holds two
chrysanthemums that also lie easily. Her dark hair is long,
it falls behind her ears, but on the left side it comes forward again over her shoulder. On her right middle finger
is a plain gold ring. On her right wrist a plain bracelet.

The Fifth Avenue photographer has stamped his
address and his advertising slogan on the cardboard backing. His slogan is "Opposite the Waldorf."

It is not a picture of innocence, it is a picture of fate.
Her dark eyes are ready for something that she could not
have known. Her brow is clear with acceptance. Her
hands lie in her lap with a composure no photographer
could have fixed. She is a nine-year-old child and she
smiles softly, but she is already caught.

Sitting there, she waits for what will come. Yet she
never meets it. For me, this child remains a being separate
from the woman I knew, this life continues unchanged,

lucid, still. Even when I was young myself, long before she died, I saw this child as someone else, not my mother when young.

2

Much ironing. She must have done just as much washing, but the ironing is what I remember, probably because she would bring the laundry into the living room of our apartment where she set up an ironing board. Tuesday afternoons when I came home from school she would be working there. I hear the small hiss as the iron met the dampened shirts, I hear the small click as she set it down on its stand. Winter afternoons, darkened early, have the smell of ironing for me; and the smell brings back a circle of lamplight, with us two and with the hushed avenue traffic outside.

One Tuesday I was late getting home. She was ironing. She asked why I was late, and I told her I had been joking around with the boys and had forgotten the time. I didn't always tell her the truth, but I did this day, I don't remember why. I thought she might be angry, and she was the parent who did the spanking. Instead, she seemed to recognize my story as if it continued one of her own.

She said that one day when she was about seventeen, she and some of her girl friends and boy friends had gone to Siegel Cooper's for ice-cream sodas, and they were coming home on the subway when one of them said something, something silly, and all of them laughed so hard and so long that they rode past their station. I tried to imagine her doing that. As she ironed, she shrugged and said, "Something, nonsense. I can't even remember what it was. But we just couldn't stop laughing."

I wished I had been there.

Many years later, twelve years after she died, there were notices in the newspapers that I was beginning a new job, and I got a letter from a man. I remembered his name; she had mentioned it sometimes. He sent congratulations, grave and warm. He wrote that he had known my mother before I was born, before she was married, he knew she was dead, and he was happy to see my news.

I wondered whether he had been on the subway that day, whether he knew what the nonsense was. I was jealous of him. His letter had the scent of ironing.

3

Earlier, when I was in kindergarten, she took me to school every day across the avenue and called for me at lunchtime. When I came out the school door and saw her face among the waiting mothers, I felt the morning change. I was no longer among equals and rivals, I was safe.

One day in the kindergarten one of the boys put some red and yellow pegs in his pocket when Miss Sprang wasn't looking. They were pegs that fit into boards on which we made designs, and they belonged to the school. The boy saw me watching him, and smirked. I felt desperate; he had done something of his own. When Miss Sprang wasn't looking, I put a handful of pegs in my pocket.

At home, when I was about to sit down to lunch, I took

the pegs out of my pocket and showed them to my mother. I didn't know what she would say, I thought she might shake her head at my naughty cleverness, but I wanted to show them to her. An adventure. I was testing something I had never tested before.

She asked me where I had got the pegs, and I told her. She whipped off her apron and grabbed me by the ear. We went out the door and down the stairs and across the street to the school, still with my ear smarting in her fingers. Miss Sprang was eating her lunch in the empty classroom, and I handed the pegs back to her. I was embarrassed because Miss Sprang was beautiful. Still I had done something. Not returning the pegs, but walking out with them.

I continued to steal for a few years, the usual boy pilferings, small change from my mother's purse, small toys from Woolworth's. Then one day when I was ten, I came home and found my mother sitting in a chair in the corner of the living room, crying. I don't know why. She looked worn. Suddenly I thought that, on that day four years before, she hadn't yanked me back to school by the ear just to discipline me. It was also to cling to something, to herself, in the midst of her own confusions. The same reason I had taken the pegs. I didn't steal much after that.

4

In little ways she tried to make me whole. After I finished college, I worked at home in a room where I kept the door locked, whether I was there or not, to separate that small space from everything else. She helped me to be separate, although she didn't entirely understand why I wanted it. She sorted out my mail in the morning and left it in front of the door of my room with a knock. She fixed meals for me at different times from the others. We rarely talked about my various likes and dislikes in the house, there was no point. She had been reared to be loyal, as she was being loyal to me by supporting my dislikes.

Her legs were getting worse. They had been going bad ever since I was a child, but, as I imagined it anyway, they had reacted to the Depression. She took treatments of various kinds, and occasionally she went to bed for a day or two. I tried not to think of the trouble she had in walking. There was nothing I could do about it, nor anyone, it seemed. Whenever she had a bad day, moving slowly, touching the wall, I looked away and thought of the small crossed slippers on the photographer's cushion. Or tried to drug my awareness of her trouble with secret doses of gratitude, for what she was doing for me.

One warm spring day I was locked in my room trying to write something. I came out late in the afternoon and saw her entering the front door, walking clumsily, carrying a couple of bags from the A & P. I took them from her and scolded her for not asking me to go to the store, though I was glad she had not bothered me. I took the bags into the kitchen. There were two other big bags from the A & P. She had already made a trip to the store, three long blocks down a hill and up again. She had not wanted to spend the money for a delivery boy and had not wanted to disturb me.

I didn't scold her. I didn't thank her. I went back into my room and locked the door and looked at whatever it was on my desk that I was writing. Nothing. Pointless. How could it be anything? Burdened thus with a blessing.

5

She got a bit loony from time to time during her long last illness. One day after she had been confined to bed for a year, I went up to visit her, as I did every week, and we talked of what I had been doing since my last visit, and relatives, and so on; then she went on talking in the same voice and told me about walking up the avenue the day before and meeting a friend of hers. I blinked, then settled and said, "How is she?" and she answered in the same matter-of-fact way. Next time I saw her, she knew very well how long she had been in bed, and had forgotten her story about the avenue. Other times she told me about meeting people in the street the day before.

She withered. There was some pain, more than some pain, but mostly she withered, upward, from those legs that had always troubled her. I liked to visit her. By going there, by sitting next to her and looking at her condensed face, by feeling her fingers clutch my hand all through the visit as if she might otherwise slip down an endless slope, by these things I could feel, for an hour or so, that I was dying with her.

A few days before the finish, clearly only a few days before, I was alone with her. She could no longer speak. I wanted to take something out of silence, I wanted to utter it, to put it in her mind, to give it to her to take even into blankness. I told her, looking at her face, what I could never have said before. About her. About being her son. Then I asked her whether she had heard, whether she understood. She blinked twice, she almost managed a nod, she made a distant reaching sound in her throat. She clutched my hand tighter.

In the car on the way to the cemetery I rode with my uncle, her brother, who was sixty-eight. He was quiet, just calm and quiet. He said, "I remember when I was seven years old, I used to sleep in the attic at the top of the house. And one morning they came up and said, 'Well, you've got a new baby sister.' " He paused. "And now."

At the graveside near me, he was still calm. He said, "Goodbye, Jeannette," and threw in a flower. He made me think that there were two in there: the withered woman and the soft, soft-eyed child who had kept her secrets.

I can't even remember the name of the cemetery, but it doesn't matter, because I never expect to go there.

Album of Older Women

1

SHE WAS TWENTY-FIVE and I was fourteen. She was a virgin and I was not. She was my high-school teacher of chemistry, the one teacher in any school who ever gave me a failing grade.

Her name was Eleanor Brophy, and she had a touch of Irish accent and a lot of Irish softness. The only time I saw her angry was when one of the boys in the class mocked something I said at the blackboard, where I was fumbling an answer, and she turned on him. My work got worse and worse through the year. I had taken chemistry because I was still obeying a willed ambition to be a doctor. The worse my work got, the more often she kept me after school for conferences. "Kauffmann," she would say, "I don't understand it. You write all those poems, but you can't remember valences."

I was writing poems and stories, some of which were published in the school magazine, and whenever she kept me to go over a wretched test paper, or even if she did not, I asked her whether she wanted to read something of mine. I did this partly as tactics, which she saw. But part of it was her gray eyes with the fierce brows so unlike her manner. She saw that, too.

She had long brown hair that she wore in a bun, and a broad brow and serene smile. Her features and her round strong neck I saw again later in the singer Flagstad. Miss Brophy was flat-chested and she moved with a somewhat

graceless pigeon-toed walk. But I couldn't imagine anything about her being different from what it was, which is
one definition of perfection.

The school was at the top of the Bronx on the edge of a
park. I lived in Manhattan. She had a new Model A Ford,
and one day after she had kept me to go over a paper, she
said she was driving downtown a bit and would give me a
lift. On the way she accidentally went through a red light.
I gloated. She laughed and blushed. "Ah, now you've got
something on me, I suppose."

I failed the state regents' exam at the end of the year,
she failed me in the course, and I had to take it again in
order to graduate the next June. The second time round
I did superbly in chemistry, as I got a sudden vision of
how it was supposed to go, basically, and everything followed easily from that. One clean autumn day she and I
walked out of school together, and she said she felt like
driving up into Westchester to see the leaves. I said impul-
sively, "Take me," and she said, "All right, Kauffmann."

Perhaps twice a month through the year we drove up
there and drove roundabout Kensico Dam and parked for
a while and talked. And laughed. In the car the world
dropped away, everything of our ages and of school. For
her birthday I gave her a poem — not of love but of
praise. For my birthday she gave me a novel.

And on my birthday I asked another present. We were
sitting in her car on a wooded road, talking and laughing,
which was all we ever did. I asked her to take down her
hair. She laughed and said, "Don't be foolish, Stanley.
What for?" "So I can see it," I said. "It's foolish," she
laughed again, and took it down. "There. What's that
now?" she asked. But she knew what it was — in the look
of it and in the meaning of the act — or she wouldn't have
done it.

Her hair was long and full, and, cloaking her shoulders, it changed her. I thought it was the most intimate thing a girl had yet done for me, though I had slept with two before that.

We laughed and teased some more, and again on other days. One day we were in the car and her hair was down and we were teasing and her face was close. Swiftly she turned her head away. I didn't kiss her, then or ever. But all at once I knew something I had never known before. I had power. Over a woman. Not just a girl, this was a woman, and I had power. I had never known that. With the two in bed in the country, I had only been the receiver of favors.

I got an almost perfect mark on the next regents' exam, and I graduated. That summer she came, with her sister, to visit me at the farm where I worked, the last summer I ever worked on a farm. In the fall I went to college and saw her a couple of times. Then I called her one day at home and her sister said she was out. A few days later I got a note from her inviting me to the Alumni Assembly, saying that she was always glad to see her former students, and she wished me well in my studies. It was the perfect teacher's note in her perfect teacher's hand.

It was a testament of fear. I was clever enough to be touched, and young enough to be proud. But I liked her so much, I was so grateful, that I never called her again.

2

In those days it was common for lower middle-class families to have maids who "slept in." New York apart-

ments often had maids' rooms and bathrooms; and immigrant girls, called greenhorns, were plentiful. Irish,
German, Polish, mostly. Some families had Negro maids,
but it took another ten years before the supply of white
girls dwindled and most of the maids were black.

So it was quite usual for an apartment to have in it an
adolescent boy, son of the family, and a young woman
who spent her nights on the premises. Stories buzzed
among the boys, most of them lies or exaggerations.

I exaggerated, too. I told my fellow thirteen-year-olds
about my wild lovemaking with Anna, our German girl.
She was a pleasant, slow farm girl, near thirty, childlike
and prudish. I explained to her in mixed German and
English that I was going to be a doctor, which I thought
was true, and that as part of my education she ought to let
me examine her, which I thought was sly. Occasionally,
when she was sure no one would come home to interrupt
and when I had flattered her sufficiently, she allowed me
various gropes and peeks.

By the time we got Polish Anna, I was fifteen and a
college freshman. She was in her mid twenties, strong and
small-breasted and sullen. The first day she was there, I
was home alone for lunch. She put a dish before me on
the table, brushing me slightly, then in the kitchen doorway, she paused and looked back. "Hey, you know, you
look like one of those movie stars," she said.

It was some sort of invitation, I supposed. What kind?
How far? "Yes? Which one?"

"That cute one. Robert Montgomery."

In the thickest fumes of adolescent fantasy, I could not
think this likely. Nobody could possibly have thought that.
Clearly there was something else involved. I felt uneasy,
incompetent.

The next afternoon, when she was fixing dinner, I went into the kitchen for a piece of fruit. When I took it out of the icebox, I looked at the pan below that caught the water from the melted ice. I was supposed to keep an eye on it, and it was nearly full. I carried it past Anna at the stove to the sink, and while I was tipping it, she grabbed my ribs hard from behind, in her ten tight fingers. "You're strong, right?" she whispered.

My mother was in the living room, not far off. I turned around to Anna, excited and scared. I didn't know what to do.

She grabbed my chin in her hand, so tightly that it hurt. "You know Bobby Berger?" she whispered.

I had never heard the name.

"He was in the place I worked six years. Fellow like you. He liked to have fun. I bet you like to have fun."

I tried to laugh carelessly, my chin still tightly in her grip.

She let me go and jabbed my chest with her fist. Close to her, I could see how beautiful her skin was, how deep and crazy her slitted eyes. "I don't like the way you got your hair cut," she whispered. "A good-looking fellow, you should cut it different. I fix it for you sometime."

I got away, out of the kitchen, and I kept away from her as much as possible the next few days. Anna said nothing to me in front of others. But when there was a chance, she gave me sullen looks, as if there were something between us. I had recently seen a movie in which a girl found out she was pregnant, and she had given looks like that to her seducer.

A few nights later I was in bed, reading. From the living room I could hear my parents' voices and the radio —that eternal radio with its comedy hours and variety hours

33

while I was trying to read or sleep. My door opened, and Anna came in.

"What's the matter?" I said.

She whispered suddenly and close. "I'm just checking up. I'm supposed to take care here, right? Make sure everything's all right?" She was next to the bed. She grabbed my chin again as I lay there. "Everything OK?"

I heard the radio and the living-room laughter. I wriggled.

"You remember Bobby Berger?" she whispered. She slid her hand under the covers. "You should talk to him, he could tell you I take care." She found what she was groping for.

The radio announcer was selling some kind of automobile. A round and cheery voice.

"Hey, come on," I whispered, "you can't — we can't —"

I felt powerless, thrilled, caught. I knew this was important, but I didn't know what to do. I heard that radio.

"You call him up, I give you the number." Her hand was still fixed under the covers. She leaned over me. I didn't know what was going to happen — to me, to my whole future. Would everything be wrecked?

Then suddenly she withdrew her hand, twisted my chin again, and went out.

I didn't sleep much that night. Prospects of orgies, true stories to tell my friends. But also sheer fright at having this girl in the house. The idea of my new, secret world of sex being discovered, impinging on the other world of my family.

I knew I couldn't handle the situation. I saw that sex always involves safety, in some degree, if one is concerned with status. One had to be able to rely on the other person, somehow. Anna promised wildness, and disgrace.

34

The next morning I asked my mother how she felt about the new maid, and she said that Anna was only fair but that she was willing to give her another week's trial. "Well," I said, "also she's — not so nice."

My mother blushed. When I came home that night, Anna was gone.

I felt relieved and elated. What a narrow escape, what a retrospective triumph. I could store this episode away, I had it, complete, it could not change for the worse. Not for the better, either, of course, but it was good enough as it was. I told all my friends that Anna had sneaked into my room every night for the five days she had been in the house, then sneaked out early in the morning. One morning my mother had discovered her leaving and had fired her on the spot. They almost believed it, I thought — they believed something, because two of them had got a glimpse of Anna one day when they called for me.

My conscience used to bother me sometimes about getting her fired, but it had all occurred too early for me. I wonder what happened to her. Something squalid or terrible, probably. Is she dead? Is she alive? — the beautiful skin gone, the crazy eyes crazier.

3

Dolly was my girlfriend's mother. They lived in a small house in a street of identical houses in a Long Island suburb, but they were very different from the neighbors. The father was English, a salesman who would have been quite successful except for the alcoholism that he had acquired in the British army, off in the colonies somewhere. Dolly had been born in Germany and had been brought here when she was ten. In her youth she had been on the operetta stage in a small way. She got her first job, as understudy, because she resembled the star of the show, a woman famous in the theater and later in films for her exquisite profile and dainty manner. The producer who hired Dolly said to the star, "This is what you looked like when I first met you." It tells almost all about Dolly to say that the star did not hate her after that introduction.

Her daughter Enid was in college, in the Dramatic Art Department, with me. She was fine and also slightly affected; and the fact that this quite consciously fine girl was devoted to me was more than my ego could bear. I bullied her a good deal of the time, and although she fought back, she never really bullied me in return. But we often had good times, and we saw each other from our sophomore year until about a year after graduation. Her eyes were her best feature, gray and superior. She had not inherited her mother's profile or figure, or the funny, delicate pathos.

I was in their home often and often spent the night there, on the sofa. I liked it best when the father was out, and when he disappeared on a week's binge, which he did every couple of months or so, I stayed there as much as I could. Dolly was wretched but somewhat liberated during those episodes. Money was especially tight during the binge weeks, but she was glad to have him out of the house. He was always very courteous to her, but she was his prisoner. She had no way of making a living, his behavior cut them off from having friends because she didn't want the neighborhood to know about his binges, and she had no relatives in this country. She stayed with him for Enid's sake, to see her through college, but she slept in Enid's room. A condition he accepted in his deferential sober weeks.

Often during the binge weeks she and Enid and I had cozy little meals at the bridge table we set up in the living room.

One summer Enid got a job as counsellor at a children's camp. I was going to stay in the city to do some work, and when I saw her off at the railroad station, she said, "Try to get out to see Dolly once in a while. She's so fond of you, and you know how things are likely to be with the pa."

I telephoned Dolly about a week later, then went out for Sunday dinner with her and Gordon. In the cooling afternoon I took her for a walk in the nearly rural streets nearby. She told me stories about her childhood in a German town, including one about the deaf old sexton named Pachs who used to fall asleep in the last row of their church during services. One Sunday near the end of the mass the priest intoned loudly, "Pax vobiscum," and the old sexton started awake, sprang to his feet, and called out, "Hier bin ich, Herr Vater." As I leaned backward with laughter, Dolly looked at me sideways like a pleased child.

She asked me to come out again in two weeks. When I got there two weeks later, about noon, I knocked on the door. No answer. I turned the knob. The door was open, and I went in. As I entered the tiny hall, the bedroom door at the top of the stairs opened, and Dolly looked out, her face tired and damp. She had evidently forgotten about me because she made a cry of surprise. Then she burst into tears and came running down the stairs into my arms. Gordon had been off drinking for about ten days, no word from him, but the checks he wrote when drunk had begun to come in and they had no money in the bank. She was practically penniless, alone — she hadn't wanted to write and upset Enid — she had mostly just been lying there, crying. Frightened.

She was wearing something thin. She was a full-bodied, very lovely woman, clinging to me.

In the years since then, I have often had fantasies in which we slipped to the floor of that little hall and, out of a huddle of emotions, made love. I know that we did not; but I still feel as if it had happened.

By and by we had sandwiches of something, and iced tea. She held my hand and apologized for being so foolish, and I held her hand and told her not to say such things. She was in her early forties, I was a college boy of eighteen, but the day was ours, as friends, as woman and man, as lovers in spirit. I thought that she knew how close we had come to making love, although there had been no overt sign. The fact that she was Enid's mother only made it more mystical and sad to me. When we went for a walk in the late afternoon, I felt as if we had returned, graver, to reality.

Gordon's binge ended, the summer ended. Eventually, after a couple of years, the affair with Enid ended — an overdue ending, considering how I treated her. When Enid told me she had begun to see someone else, the first thing I thought of was my pride, which was proof enough that she was right to break it off. The second thing I thought of was that day with Dolly; and that there would never be another.

4

I was the best senior student in the directing class so I got the annual plum. Each year an exclusive girls' finishing school in Connecticut did a play, and each year they asked the head of the Dramatic Art Department at my college to recommend a student of his to direct their show. In my senior year he recommended me, and I felt imperial. The fee was a hundred dollars and expenses — in 1935. Up at that school I met Mireille.

They were very careful of their girls. Boys were rarely allowed on the school grounds. All the male parts in their plays were performed by girls, and besides there was a faculty member present every time I rehearsed. Just because I was there, nineteen and appreciative. Like so many of the rich, this school was stingy. Instead of buying copies of the published play for the cast, they typed up copies. The play they had chosen was Barrie's *Quality Street,* and at the casting tryout, we read through the typescripts in the presence of a caricature schoolmistress, black throat-band and all. We came to the stage direction: "She runs to the window to peep between the curtains." The typist had left the final *p* off "peep." There were strangulated giggles in the presence of the granite teacher, and I concentrated as hard as I could on my hundred dollars.

At the first rehearsal, the faculty proctor was the French teacher, Mademoiselle Parlier. She was in her early thirties, long-nosed, full-bosomed, long-waisted, and small. She wore a shirtwaist with flowing sleeves and a dark velvet tam. I thought she looked like the heroine of a French film, very real. After we were introduced, I turned to work and worked hard for about three hours.

I had to be taken to the railroad station after every session — I went up there twice a week from the city — and this day Mademoiselle Parlier offered me a lift. As we drove, I could tell from her manner that she had been impressed with my work. I was flattered, but I had no kind of intention toward her, I had no thought of it. She seemed unattainable; French; perhaps thirty-five. Besides, I didn't want to risk that money.

We chatted, and in the course of the chat, I presumed to ask her first name. She said, "One that you have never heard. Mireille." I had been given a present, a golden chance. I said, "Isn't that the name of an opera by Gounod?" She was as impressed as I had hoped, and said, "You are the first one in this country who has ever heard of it."

In a moment we turned into another road, and she said, "I live just there, a little cottage. Do you have time for a cup of tea? My English habit. I acquired it there. Shall we have some?" I was happy, nothing more, and as there was another train in about an hour, I said yes.

It was a pretty house with flowers, and a low-ceilinged living room with a piano and a violin and art books and French paperbound volumes all over. She made tea, and we smoked and talked for a while, very cozily. Then she took me to the station.

At the next rehearsal she was the proctor again, again in the velvet tam. "I have told the headmistress that I do not mind attending the repetitions, I am interested in the progress of the play," she said. I forgot her again during the rehearsal, then again she offered me a lift. Again, we turned into her road, she asked me whether I had time for tea and I accepted. And again I had no kind of intention toward her. But I knew later — anyway I know now — that she had made up her mind about me on the first day, that the first invitation had been to give her the chance to see whether she could rely on my discretion and the second invitation was because she had decided.

Again we had tea, and I loved my new state. I was almost finished with college, conversing easily about books and life with a Frenchwoman in her art-filled cottage.

It was time to go, and I asked whether I might use the bathroom. She said it was through the bedroom. I went through and closed the bathroom door. When I came out, the bedroom shades were drawn, the bedroom door was closed. She was inside, leaning against the door, naked.

What I remember more strongly than my surprise or excitement is the look on her face as she came toward me. Something like hatred. I tried to think it was hunger only, but there was hatred in it. It was marvelous to me. New.

I took a much later train, and every rehearsal day after that, I took that later train. I had never felt anything like this, so immersed. I had slept with girls, I had used the word "love," but it was the first time I had felt drowned with a woman, grateful for the drowning.

After five weeks, the play was performed one afternoon. The headmistress and the parents were very pleased, and there were compliments over the punch. Then Mireille drove me to the station again, and again I took the later train. At the station, in her car, as the train arrived, I said I would telephone her the following week. I wanted it never to end, and anyway I assumed she would be wounded if I did not make some sort of promise. I had no clear idea how it could continue, but that didn't matter at the moment. She said, "Yes, do. Do telephone."

That was a Friday. I called her on Monday afternoon, ready to spend some of my hundred dollars on a hotel room if she could come to New York or on train fare to go up there. She said, "Oh, dear, there are some friends here now. Could we speak tomorrow?" I called the next day, and she said that she wasn't planning to visit New York that week, she was busy with end-of-year affairs; so I couldn't come up there either. I was baffled but tried to write it off as mood. I called again the following week and she very nearly hung up on me. She was much more remote than on the day we had first met. I tried frantically to close the distance over the telephone, but it was ice all the way. She cut off the talk.

I didn't call again. It wasn't my pride, I was ready to be humbled, but I felt that she wasn't even sufficiently interested to humble me. She had cut it.

I couldn't understand. The woman with whom — until two weeks before — the bed had been a universe. Then I remembered the first bedroom day and the look on her face. I supposed that the finish had been in the beginning.

What love might be, I did not yet really know, but I saw now that romance was a male invention, licensed by women and sometimes pitied by them.

TWO

Album of a Director

1

I<small>N THE LATE SUMMER</small> OF 1962, coming back from Canada to Manhattan, I drove into the past. I had just spent a few days at the Shakespeare Festival in Ontario, and now, as I came down through central New York, I began to see place names that touched my own Shakespeare theater. Twenty-five years earlier I had scuttled through these towns in summertime putting up posters for productions. In those days I had always approached these towns from the south. Driving down from the north, I hadn't realized that I was getting so near to The Palace Wood.

My last summer there had been in 1940. One is not supposed to revisit: neither the place nor one's self can be the same. Just for that reason I swung off the highway toward the lake road, hoping to diminish my memory of it.

After a few miles I saw a poster. This week they were playing a musical, a Broadway hit of a few years before. I enjoyed that, grimly. I enjoyed seeing the flashy title of that flashy show under the same old logo, "The Palace Wood," and under the logo Peter Quince's line: "Meet me in the palace wood, a mile without the town."

Then the name of the director. I enjoyed that, too. His first name was Buzz.

There was the big old house, on a rise along the lake-side road. There, behind it, was the theater, built on a bank with a brook running below. On the other side of

45

the theater had once been a green knoll on which we had done outdoor performances. The knoll had been leveled, the place graveled for a parking lot.

It was midafternoon. Five or six people straggled out of the theater, apparently after a rehearsal, talking and teasing. They seemed just as young as we had been, but sillier. Nowadays young people often seem much more mature than I was at their age, but not these.

I decided to go to the show that night, to revel in rue and bile. After I had bought a ticket, I told the two women in the box office that I had been a member of the theatrical company that built the place. At first they seemed puzzled, as if I had said I had been a member of Columbus's crew. Then they exclaimed various exclamations. I had mentioned it only because I wanted permission to poke around backstage for a bit. I asked, and they chirped agreement. (It was twenty years later, but what were *they* doing there?) They took me around back. I couldn't get rid of them. There was only one thing I really wanted to see, and they were with me when I saw it.

On the back wall of the stage, the first day we rehearsed there, we had all signed our names with indelible pencil right on the wood. With the date, a day in early July of 1937. Then the signatures had been shellacked over, to preserve them.

All there. All still there. There was my name. And here was the subsequent I, looking at it.

I had to do something with the women looking on. I laughed affectionately for my youth.

When I got back in the car, I almost tore up the ticket for that night, but I thought it would be too conscious a gesture, done for a nonexistent movie camera. Besides, I was sure that the show would be terrible. It was, as I was later happy to see. I left in the intermission.

2

I was so young when I went to college — fifteen, in 1931 — that my mother took me to the first interview. I was so young that I didn't mind. I wanted to major in Dramatic Art, as the department was named. My parents had agreed with surprising ease, but my mother had insisted on coming with me to the first interview to see what the place was like. The building was on Washington Square. The department office was on an upper floor, just next to a small theater. The chairman was CD, who had a cigarette between his teeth when I met him.

His office had two small rooms, the secretary's and his own. The walls of both were covered with signed and framed photographs of actors and other theater people, many of them retired or dead, some of them already legendary to me. I was impressed with CD in advance.

When he came out and saw my mother, he took the cigarette out of his mouth and, in what I learned was a characteristic way, he put out his hand warmly as he pulled his head back benignly. He was tall and slightly soft in outline, slightly round-shouldered, slightly paunchy. He was dimly red-headed, and bald on top. He wore brown-rimmed eyeglasses. He had high cheekbones, small eyes, and a pencil-line mouth. A few years afterward, an interviewer compared his face to Edwin Booth's, which pleased him a lot. But it was nonsense: the one famous actor whom he resembled, and strikingly, was Henry Irving.

My mother was impressed, I was accepted into the department, I started school and fell into heaven. I have never been happier than I was some of the time in college. Some of the dull times came about because of courses that I needed for my degree and that didn't interest me. More of the unhappiness was caused by my happiness, my single-minded, almost manic happiness — when I didn't get preferments I wanted in the work I was manic about, when my ego was chafed, when I thought my uniqueness and excellence were ignored, when I saw that some of that excellence was not what I had thought it. In acting, for instance. But to be in that school, to be in that department, was happiness. I gobbled the department courses as quickly as they would let me; I reveled in reading about the theater. The books in the college library were not enough. In those days there was a small separate room in the old Fifty-eighth Street Public Library, a rectangle walled from floor to ceiling with shelves of theater books. During my four college years I read enough of those books so that I could say loosely that I had read them all. And just outside that room were many, many shelves of plays that I wound through like a boa.

Very soon in my first year CD became aware of me in his classes in more than the obligatory way, aware through my papers, my questions, my laughter at his jokes that not everyone got, my own facetiousness at which everyone laughed except him — and even then he teasingly overdid the stone face.

And soon, since he was the pope of everything I cared about, he became all-powerful to me. He often wore crepe-soled shoes. I would calculate how to pass him in the hall as he splayfooted along in squishes. I hoped for either a smile or a cold nod, as long as it came from him.

I was fifteen. He was forty-two.

His courses were Appreciation of the Drama, which, in

spite of its ladies-club title, was a treatment of theater esthetics that shook me as if there were hands on my shoulders; History of the Theater; several years of Shakespeare; a year of Modern Drama, notorious in the university for its anti-Ibsen prejudice; and a seminar in directing. I took all these courses in time, and I was the reason that, in my last year, he formed a small tutorial group of playwrights.

In May, at the end of my first year, when I arrived at the exam room for the Appreciation final, he asked me to stop by his office after I had finished. When I did, he looked through the bundle of blue exam books on his desk, extracted my three books, and handed me all the others. "Please read them and grade them for me," he said coolly. "I'm too busy. In confidence, of course." I was in restrained ecstasy. I was sixteen.

But I was worried about my own exam. I had dug so deeply into the first two questions that I had barely started on the third of the five questions when the exam period ended. I told CD. He picked up my blue books, riffled some pages, and frowned. "I can't read your damned handwriting anyway," he said and wrote a neat little *A* on the first page. "All right," he said, dismissing me with a nod. I would have walked through the wall if the door hadn't opened easily.

The chief business of the department was training actors. That's why I had gone there. A lot of other theater courses were required, but they all fed the idea of training actors in a university. Playwriting and other plans came later for me. Already at other universities there were theater schools training playwrights and directors and designers and technicians as well as actors. This department was for actors.

Every Friday afternoon some of the students performed one-act plays for other students and the faculty.
Long before the exam business, three months after I entered the school, I was in one of those Friday afternoon
bills. It was a short play by Paul Hervieu, and all I remember of it was that I wore a gray moustache. I hoped
for some kind of jubilation from CD afterward. He said
only that I had showed "agreeable reticence." It was not
the comment I had dreamed of, but it exhilarated me. It
sounded so pithy, so knowledgeable. It was better than
gush.

And a month or so after that, when I had been in the
school only half a year, something happened that changed
my life. I still think that, outside my personal life, it's the
most influential thing that has happened to me. CD invited me to work with the Village Players. Not knowing it
at the time, I handed him the next ten years. But that, as
it turned out, was part of the eventual disappointment,
that it was only ten years: I came to hope that I had
handed him the rest of my life.

This theater group was not the Village Players that everyone had heard of and is now marked in the histories.
That was an earlier company, begun just after the First
War, which had played in Greenwich Village and had
then moved up to Broadway where it changed its name.
CD had founded his own group about five years before I
arrived, and it was characteristic of him that he insisted on
the name Village Players because it was appropriate and
that he almost resented the fact that the earlier group had
used it before he came along. Anyway he thought they
had lost all title to the name by reason of their change, although in fact he got their formal consent. And to cap it,
he put responsibility for distinction between the two
groups on the public, as if it were their duty to be suf-

ficiently interested to understand. Even today when people hear that I was once with the Village Players they wonder how I can be old enough to have started with some of its famous alumni; or else they assume that I *am* old enough.

That was only the first chore in explaining the group. The big one was how the company related to the university. (Among ourselves it was always the company: we never called it anything else.) We performed, every weekend through the season, in one or the other of two theaters at the university, except when we were hired to play at some school in the metropolitan area. CD, the director of the company, was also the head of the Dramatic Art Department in the university, and some of the actors were on the faculty. Other actors were graduates of the department. A few third- or fourth-year students were invited to work with the company. (I was an ego-blowing exception.) But it was not a university function. It was separately operated and differently intended. It was independent: the university gave it no money. The other way round — out of its receipts the company paid rent for the theaters. The company owned its costumes and lights and drapes and such scenery as was used. In time we even rented a rehearsal and prop-building studio of our own a few blocks away.

It was a repertory company, mostly of Shakespeare. And it was really repertory: once a production was added, it was rarely dropped, although casts would alter. If a play hadn't been done in a year or two, it could still be brought back with a week's rehearsal. In time there were some Sheridan and Goldsmith and Shaw plays, even two by me. The idea was to continue; to build; to blend a style; and to use the university as a base for doing it.

To me it seemed a wonderful idea, seemed so immediately, in a high cloudy idealistic way. It was a blow against the dailiness of life around me. Already that life seemed to me divided, in classic American schema, between the pure and the commercial; and, because this company essentially looked backward, in its organization as well as its choice of plays, looked toward the past as something purer than the present that ought to be revived, it struck my romantic spirit strongly. I wanted, before I was asked, to devote myself to it like a lay monk. It was a vocation and a refuge.

I don't mock the idea of the company now. It *was* wonderful, one wonderful idea about the theater. It was lopsided, I came to see, because of CD, but because of CD it existed at all and, like him, it was unique and partially wonderful. It enabled me to spend ten years in a world that, within its constrictions, was magically nourishing. When I left, after ten years, I figured that I had taken part, one job or another, in almost two hundred performances each of *A Midsummer Night's Dream* and *As You Like It* and *Macbeth* (our most popular plays), over a hundred and fifty of *Hamlet,* many dozens of performances of *Julius Caesar* and *Twelfth Night* and *Romeo and Juliet.* And the other plays. It was not a thoroughly wasteful way to spend one's youth.

The company gave me the feeling of entering a neglected mainstream of tradition. A few years after I joined, CD decided to add *The Taming of the Shrew* to the repertory. Our costumes for this play, the only ones not specifically made for us, were donated by the actress Margaret Anglin from her production of twenty years before. My skinny self, as Vincentio, fit into a costume with the name-tag of Sydney Greenstreet. I felt hereditarily confirmed by stepping into a costume from the past, a costume that had once been worn by a now-noted fat actor when he was thin.

Nobody in the company got paid. We played almost every Friday night and Saturday afternoon, sometimes also on Saturday night, from September to June. (We rehearsed every other night of the week except Sunday.) We had fair attendance, sometimes sellouts to high schools. All receipts went to the company, for the costumes and scenic pieces and lights and rent to the university. The members were expected to support themselves otherwise. The model was the Abbey Theater, whose people had worked at other jobs for a living long after the Abbey was famous.

When I started with the company, the repertory was small, the goals were set. The repertory grew; the plans changed, for a time, largely because of me.

All that was ahead. Now I was merely a first-year student, not a fledged member of the company, chosen to play a small part. Within the school I was much less hated than I would have expected. Most of the students thought that if CD had tapped a freshman, there must be something pretty nifty about him.

I found out very quickly what a fifteen-year-old does in a Shakespeare company — he plays old men. My first part was Adam in *As You Like It,* and when CD asked me to learn it, he said, "You know it's the part that Shakespeare himself played?" I didn't, but I took it as further confirmation of the laying-on of hands.

The play had been in repertory for a couple of years. One actor had gone to Hollywood to be a screenwriter, another actor was shifted out of Adam, and I was put in it, in a going production. The Rosalind, who gave me friendly but place-putting smiles, was by day a department store junior executive. The Orlando was one of my acting teachers. I must have done all right because after a couple of rehearsals, CD issued me the costume, complete with cowl. Oh, those cowls. How many I wore, as different old men, during the next ten years. I was pretty good at makeup even before I went to drama school, through lots of amateur acting, and I soon got better through a course there. I made my own white beard for Adam.

My first appearance with the company was not in one of our university theaters. We were engaged to do *As You Like It* for one performance at a settlement house on the East Side. Each of us was given a typed instruction sheet with the time and place and directions to the place. Only a few years ago I threw out my old tin makeup box; on the bottom, stained with spirit gum, was that onionskin instruction sheet, dated March 10, 1932.

Our host at the settlement house was the head of their theater activities, Mrs. Richard Mansfield, widow of the turn-of-the-century star, who had been her husband's leading lady. She was now a small, white-haired woman with a round face and a round hat. I was introduced to her after the performance. She smiled sweetly and said, "Ah, yes, Adam. Did you know that Shakespeare used to play that part himself?"

3

I graduated in 1935 with a good warped education. I had learned a lot about what interested me, much less about most other subjects. In music and English courses I had done well, but what saved me in the other required work was a virtuoso memory. For instance, I had done nothing at all through the second half of second-year German, but the day before the exam I memorized our main text, Schiller's *Maria Stuart,* in English — the whole play. Passages for translation would be half the exam. I scored perfectly on that half and scratched enough on the rest to squeeze through.

On the other hand I was stuffed with theater history and theater biography and criticism, with plays of every era. I had loved every course in the department, even Mise en Scène. (For our final "paper" each of us had to bring in complete production plans and designs for Schnitzler's *Green Cockatoo.* My costume designs may be the only ones ever drawn with a ruler.) And the most important event in my life had grown in its importance: I had become a member of the company.

There was no ceremony about it, there certainly wasn't any voting, not in any group run by CD. I merely noted that, after a certain time — I think during my third year — my name appeared on the back of the program in the roster of members. I thanked CD, who put out his hand and put his head back benignly and said, "Very pleased to have you. To celebrate." He gave me a cigar.

Membership meant that, instead of being a fill-in, a student apprentice, I was taken to be permanently valuable to a group that intended to be permanent. I felt my life sliding onto an ascending highway. CD had never asked me about it; he had assumed from my attitude toward the company that I felt I had found a home. I took it as a compliment that I hadn't been asked, that my bonding had been assumed.

I played and kept playing, always played, small parts.

Many of them were old men, with cowls. All the members shared the stage management and other chores, but those who played the smaller parts in any show, as I did in all shows, did most of those chores. I was often the stage manager, and I could very soon run my shows without promptbook, every line in my head, every light cue and music cue. I was beginning to design some of the lighting, and I was doing most of the music — which meant selecting portions of phonograph records and playing them on CD's big Capehart which had to be lugged from his apartment across the street for every dress rehearsal and performance, then returned. Backstage, I often worked in the dark — in *Macbeth,* for instance, so that no light would leak through the drapes onto the darkened stage — one hand on light-dimmers, the other on the volume knob of the phonograph to fade the music in or out, and all this in makeup and costume.

More plays were slowly but continually added to the repertory, their rehearsals interwoven with those of our previous plays that had to be brushed up. So this meant that through my last college years, in addition to classes, I spent a good portion of most days with or around CD.

When he was directing, he had two favorite places in which to work, very close or very far. When the play was new or he was rehearsing someone new in a role, he would sit on a chair on the stage at the front, watching like a conductor, almost shaping things by hand. Most of the time he would sit far back in the theater, rarely interrupting, coming up after a scene or two to make comments. Except in the warmest months, he usually sat with his overcoat over his shoulders, a cigarette between his teeth or sometimes a cigar in his hand. I, very often the stage manager, would be sitting with the promptbook at a desk in front of the stage and, whether he was working near or far, heard everything.

CD himself acted some parts, ones that required a convincing middle age, which is much more difficult for young actors than old age, or ones that he simply wanted to play: Macbeth, Malvolio, Jaques, William the Waiter in *You Never Can Tell.* CD's own mentor, an English actor who had died in 1923, had played William under Shaw's direction, and when we did the play, CD felt an apostolic commitment to the part although he had nothing like the necessary geniality. When he was acting, the stage manager stood in for him at many rehearsals so that he could watch from the front. I got to do Jaques's Seven Ages speech a good deal because CD was always fussing with the foresters' reactions in that scene and wanted to see it from the front.

I take it as a control in my judgment of CD, an index that I can rely on my high opinion of him in other ways, that I never thought much of him as an actor, even when I was youngest and freshest with him. He was a careful technician: he never made a slovenly move, never fractured a line of verse, never muddied a meaning, but he had no warmth, no power. He showed you, fairly skillfully, what the man was thinking or feeling, but it rested there: you were shown. Sometimes, as in the most terrible moments of Macbeth, I felt that he wanted to crack through, that he was straining to strip himself, but it never happened. He was best in mannered comedy like Malvolio, where what he could do with his brain took care of almost everything.

As for his directing and the style in which he tried to train us and unify us, they were the traditional triumphant. I don't think CD ever had a truly original idea in

57

directing; I don't think he ever made a stupid or clumsy comment. (Until near the end.) His ideal was to preserve and carry forward the best of the theater's past, as he had gathered it from years of playgoing, from endless study of promptbooks, from endless readings of theater histories and actors' biographies. He had thick looseleaf notebooks full of passages from theater books that he had marked as he read them and that had been typed up by his secretary, passages about the art of acting or the ways in which scenes or characters had been played. All this was capped by what he had learned from the old English actor who had played for Shaw. CD had put a plaque to his teacher on the wall of our smaller theater with the Shakespeare tag: "There are no tricks in plain and simple faith." This old actor's parents had been a famous acting-producing pair in mid-Victorian England, the son had himself worked with the great in London and New York at the turn of the century, and CD had studied much of Shakespeare with him in his later years. CD, who preferred cigarettes, smoked cigars some of the time because his teacher had done so. I saw stage photos of the Englishman that showed why CD held a cigar butt upward.

CD was no pedant, he was a passionate conservative. He fought against what he took to be decay, of technique and of taste. He was trying to revive what he thought was health, the theater he had seen in hs youth, had heard about from his elders, had read about in histories. He was interested only in theater art — he ridiculed most academic teachers of Shakespeare — but he faced backward to see it. The only new Shakespeare production I ever heard him say a good word about, other than some of our own, was *Richard II* with Maurice Evans, which was cut from a cloth he admired. When Orson Welles came along and began to rocket, CD always referred to him grinningly as Whoreson Welles. Still his credo was a credo, not antiquarian dust. Once he told me that, when he was in college, he had undergone a serious operation after he had been warned that his chances were only a bit better than even. "But," he said, and I believed him, "I had just seen Forbes-Robertson's Hamlet fifteen times, and I didn't much care."

He was gravely courteous to women, chaffingly courteous to girls. I thought then, with admiration, that here too he was maintaining a tradition. In his direction of actresses he never seemed to me to have much sexual charge, but he had a sense of romance. He adored Julia Marlowe, the retired Shakespearean star, whom he knew. Whenever she was in New York and invited him to tea at her hotel, he wore a wing collar for the visit.

With men, his behavior was, I thought, equally in an old style. He had a belief in male friendship that was already a bit archaic. He was unmarried, and he seemed to me a bachelor out of an age when that word and idea were really in use, when bachelorhood meant wood-paneled clubs and late-night male suppers and walking trips with chums and elaborate practical jokes. There was something gentlemanly about it to me.

But he came from no kind of elegant background. He was the son of Irish-Scotch farm people, from middle New York State. His sister, who was older, was married to a carpenter up there. He had a "fat brother," as he always called him, with whom he had once managed a baseball team up there. His speech still had touches of the rural. The word "horse" always had a special rustic fold on the *r*. Once he gave our Portia a reading of the line, "I pray you, tarry," and later she asked me privately, "Does he really want me to say 'terry'?"

4

The more I learned from CD and worked with the company and learned of the theater's past, the more I wanted the company to be my future. The more I believed in the company principles, the safer I felt with them wrapped around me and the less I wanted to spend time at anything else. The mere fact of my graduation would make no difference in the centering of my life. I wanted the company to take even more of my time after graduation than it had been taking. I wanted the company to move from its university setting to a being of its own and to grow in recognition. My best friends in the company felt the same.

One day in CD's office during my last year in school we were talking about the old days, his old days. As an adolescent in his upstate town he had played Donalbain for two performances when Modjeska had come barnstorming through as Lady Macbeth. He had spent every possible moment in the wings listening to her, and he could imitate her, complete with delicate Polish accent. It was late afternoon as we talked, that lazy time of surging feelings at the end of a day. I felt linked. I wanted never to leave this atmosphere, the company of a man who had touched the receding past and who wanted to keep it from receding, wanted to carry the best of it on. I took a leap. I told CD what I had been thinking about the company, how I wanted it to march forward from a beautiful enterprise that we supported to a beautiful enterprise that could support us. So that I could give it all my time. I told him that all I was doing really was persisting in ideas that he had taught me. I would never be much of an actor — he had convinced me of that. I simply wanted to put my life in the company: to play such parts as I could, stage-manage, write plays for the company occasionally, possibly some time in the future even direct.

He listened very attentively, leaning back in his chair, his hands clasped behind his bespectacled head. He pursed his thin mouth, then he said, "Yes. You're the only one who could take over. You're the only one with the vision."

Even today, writing the words, I feel the pang of pride, the wonderful ache of a limitless future.

He never repeated that remark to anyone that I know of, nor did I. Nor did he ever say it again to me. But he said it then. And later he and I often talked between ourselves and with other members about some of the ideas I had raised that afternoon: a move away from the university base, into a full-time life, into self-sufficiency. Some of the people in the company were too tied with obligations, too settled in jobs, to consider such a move. For me, for most of the younger members, who were most of the members, it seemed just a matter of time before we found the means to move. Probably, I measured it secretly, only a few years after I graduate.

My parents, even though these were black Depression days, grumbled very little at my unconventional and, to them, wispy plans: at least they understood why my time was used as it was, four nights a week for rehearsals and weekends for performances. Other people, relatives, and friends, shrugged, as if I were eccentric or going through growing pains. (I was only nineteen when I graduated.)

Most of the girls I knew either were involved with the company, like Enid who was my "steady," or were a bit starry-eyed because I was a member.

So I didn't look for any other kind of career when I graduated. I didn't want to get entangled or lie too much to employers. I had a few odd impermanent jobs that didn't entail commitment to the boss. I wrote a lot of things and sold a few. I squirmed along in money terms, meanly and grubbily, with no kind of bohemian joy in grubbiness, with worn clothes and with small change in my pockets. A dollar bill was something of a thrill.

I spent much of my time with CD, although no more than he spent with other men in the company outside rehearsals. He spent almost no time with women, alone or in groups. I went up to his penthouse apartment across from the university only by invitation or after a telephone inquiry, but I went quite a lot. It always excited me to be invited up for a drink after rehearsal, either with or without others. Sometimes on a boring Sunday, after a week spent more or less with him, I telephoned him from home and was sometimes asked to come down for an hour.

And sometimes I was invited to stay overnight, to sleep on the sofa in the living room, although my home was only half an hour away. There was never any real need to stay, but once in a long while CD would say, always abruptly and brusquely, "It's late. You may as well bunk down on the sofa if you like." I would always accept, would call my mother and tell her that we had been working and that I was needed early in the morning.

I felt privileged whenever I was with him. He was, stubbornly and somewhat haughtily, what I wanted to be in the theater and much of what I wanted to be as a man: wise, skilled, stoic, courteous, Roman. Away from him I

parroted him in manner and even used some of his anec-
dotes as my own. I couldn't smoke cigarettes, as he did
much of the time — I had a pipe — but I liked cigars, and
very rarely he gave me one of his. It was always, as when
I'd thanked him for taking me into the company, some
sort of occasion. His cigars were no better than the ones I
bought once in a while, but they tasted better. ("No cigar
ever made was worth more than a nickel" was one of the
worst pieces of pseudo wisdom I ever had from him.)

Preparatory hours I felt them, preparatory to a great,
shaped, aspiring life, when I was in his apartment, sitting
across from this big pasty-faced man with slit eyes and a
fringe of dirty red hair around his bald pate, as he leaned
back in the green-cushioned Morris chair he had inherited from his English mentor, a drink on the flat arm
of it, and in his light baritone read to me, to us if there
were others — Shakespeare or old poets—or told stories
or read from books on mysticism — Ouspensky and Brag-
don — to which he professed to subscribe. Of course I can
see now, it's easy to see now, that, outside the theater
where his conservatism had purpose and was lit by his talent, he was a very narrow man, full of social and political
pronouncements that were ignorant and bigoted. I can
see that his views of women were both sentimental and
dirty. At the time I could see his narrowness, but I
thought it his way of discrimination, somehow aristocratic;
and though we always disagreed politically — he called
me a Red because I liked Roosevelt and read socialist liter-
ature — I liked our disagreements because they formed
still a different kind of tie with him. As for his comments
on women, with their lofty worldliness and gold-toothed
chuckles, they seemed to admit me to a club of grownups.

Everyone has had at least one teacher who meant a

great deal to him. The difference here was that I expected to be with CD for life.

There was another oddity. In spite of everything between us, I knew that he didn't really like me. He admired
me in several ways, he had some expectation of me, he
praised much of my writing, and from time to time, because of these things, I felt a small glow of affection from
him. But in any quick and spontaneous way, he didn't
respond to me as he did to some of the other people in
the company.

Partly this was my fault. I had decided through my
progress in all my schools and adulation from past
teachers, through early publication in lots of little magazines, and of course through my early acceptance into the
company, that I was some sort of superior person, the superiority not yet specified but nevertheless certain. My
conviction of this often made me arrogant or facetious,
both of which must have been hard to take.

But mostly CD's fundamental reaction to me was chemi-
cally instantaneous, not caused by this or that action. In
an almost primal animal way, he was never completely
unguarded with me even when he was closest and most
affectionate. Besides, he had a strong residue of rural
anti-Semitism. He was teaching in a university with many
Jewish students, so it was meant as a special mark of favor
to me, as one of them, if he made a small anti-Jewish
crack in private. I laughed at his anti-Jewish cracks because I valued the implication that I was "not like them."
It was an ambition of many American Jews in those days,
particularly of my generation, to be "not like them." I
meant the laughter, I felt only the slightest twinge of dis-
comfort far back in my mind. Still the communion didn't
bring CD and me as close as he was with others, some of

64

whom too were Jewish but about whom he was in no way wary.

His feelings about Jews had a funny side because of his connection with Boris Kraft. In the then-flourishing Yiddish theater in downtown New York, Kraft was a powerful figure, one of the most powerful actors I have seen in any language. I knew virtually no Yiddish — it was scorned in my Germanic family — but when I saw Kraft in his own Second Avenue theater, I knew he was a king in his palace, appearing to his people.

A few years before I came along, Kraft had engaged CD to work with him on Shylock in English. A vaudeville circuit had offered Kraft a contract to tour a half-hour version of the Shylock scenes from *The Merchant of Venice*. Somehow he had heard of CD and engaged him as coach. Kraft became CD's idolater and soon asked him to play Antonio on the tour: and CD found time to do it for a while. (He had done some odd things before I knew him — among them, the villainous Dr. Wu in a radio series. He would point to things in his apartment that he had bought with his radio money. "My Dr. Wu bookcase." "My insidious Oriental piano.")

Kraft had once said that CD looked "like the son of a distinguished rabbi," and CD used to laugh at that remark with me. He couldn't understand it, nor could I. But he liked his association with Kraft, I think, because it both pardoned and amused his quasi-secret anti-Semitism.

Kraft always invited him to new productions at his theater. One Sunday night in my last year at college CD asked me to go with him to see Kraft's new revival of one of his old repertory pieces. I was delighted. There was a great fuss over CD in the front of the house. The box-office treasurer summoned the house manager who summoned the managing director who ushered us to choice seats in the crowded, noisy theater.

The play was a comedy set in an old eastern European village, obviously a staple because the audience laughed with the relish of the familiar rather than with surprise. Kraft played a wizened old rabbi in fur-trimmed hat, velvet breeches, white stockings, and silver-buckled pumps. At one point the moon came down. He grabbed it, and it started to rise again, carrying him. His legs spread wide in fear, and the audience howled. The last time I had seen Kraft before that, in another old Yiddish play, he had frightened me cold with his fury.

After the performance we were told that "the great man," as CD called him, was awaiting us. We were escorted backstage, and his dresser admitted us. Kraft had taken off his wig and beard and costume and was sitting before his mirror in his makeup and his BVDs. He rose and took CD's hand in both of his and bowed low in his BVDs. When I was introduced, he gave my hand a perfunctory shake, then continued talking to CD. What impressed me most was Kraft's barrel-chested dignity, standing there in his ridiculous underwear, his face covered with yellow paint and penciled wrinkles. While he and CD were talking, there was a knock at the door, and the dresser brought in a girl, a dancer in the large company. She was evidently asking, in Yiddish, whether she could be excused from a rehearsal the next day. Kraft, no more disturbed by his undress than she was, thought about it regally, then gave permission. She thanked him respectfully and left. We sat, and the dresser served us all thimbles of slivovitz. Kraft, still in underwear and paint, told CD of a contract that he had just been offered by a big film studio; he said that, if he accepted, he hoped that CD could come to Hollywood for a time and coach him. CD, with the senatorial majesty that he could achieve at will, nodded graciously and said he hoped so, too: he would be happy to be of use again to such an artist as Kraft.

When we left, I was tingling. To have been there with those two men at that meeting! What possible importance the meeting could have I wasn't sure, but it was those two men, talking professionally. I didn't want to break out of that atmosphere: I walked CD to his apartment house fifteen minutes away. He, too, was apparently feeling exhilarated. At the door he said, "I feel like reading aloud for a bit. You can come up if you want to." Of course I wanted to. As he unlocked his apartment door, he looked at his watch and said, "It'll be late before long. You might want to stay over. In which case you'd better phone your parents now." Of course I telephoned — my poor mother was used to these calls around midnight — and said I wouldn't be home to sleep, there were things I had to talk about with CD.

He sank into his Morris chair with a drink and some books. He pushed his brown-rimmed glasses lower. He read some poems. I smoked a pipe and listened. He read from old copies, full of notes, books that he had used as a student at Columbia. They seemed to me crusted with riches.

In that penthouse apartment the night closed tightly around us like a fist, condensing the space. CD's brass gooseneck reading lamp became a circle of light within a circle of black. He finished the fifth or sixth poem — Tennyson's "Ulysses," one of his favorites — and closed the book. He seemed just slightly uneasy, instead of in his usual fairly cool command. Just slightly. It crossed my mind that if we were two other people, this might be the moment when the teacher made a sexual advance toward the student. I knew what homosexuality was. I knew it existed, but that was all. There was no question of tolerating it in friends; the subject never arose, whatever secret lives there may have been. It was never talked about except scoffingly or, at best, pityingly. In my own life, all it meant was a contradistinction to healthy male companionship and affection, but it had nothing to do with my life or the lives around me as far as I was aware. All of us knew that CD had no women friends except the wives of friends, that he often had young men staying in his apartment. But the men were mostly members of the company, as far from homosexuality as I was, or former students who now lived out of town and stayed with him when they came to the city. None of us speculated much about CD's sex life. Once in a great while he would give us the gold-toothed grin and say something about "pajama parties," and that seemed to me maturely wicked and conclusive. The idea that CD could be homosexual — a condition I associated honorably only with the past, with Julius Caesar or Michelangelo — was not conceivable to me. It would have shocked me greatly. It would have changed my cosmos.

Still the thought crossed my mind at that moment, as a possibility for two other people; and I felt that he had felt the same flash and knew that I had felt it. But I thought that it had affected him the same way: only as recognition of how apt the moment would have been for two others.

Absolutely nothing happened. He gestured toward the bathroom and said, "You'd better get along and wash while I make up the sofa." When I came out of the bathroom, the sheets and blanket and pillow were all in place and his bedroom door was closed. When I woke the next morning, he was making breakfast for us. He peered over his glasses at me. "Bacon's done, eggs will be ready in a few minutes." In the daylight there was no touch of that late-night feeling.

But I knew that it had happened, and I was sure that he knew. In the morning I thought that, if a move had been made the night before, I would have been horrified. I might easily have said so simple-minded a thing as "But, professor, what about Enid?" She was not only my "steady," she was in the company.

Now I think I only thought those things the next day to protect myself. If there had been a move toward me that night, I might at that moment have thought it was right to happen, that it had been considered for me and found right. I had trusted this man with so much that I probably would also have trusted him in that. Now I think that the only reason it did not happen was that fundamentally he didn't like me.

If it had happened, my whole life might have been different: not perhaps because of one homosexual experience, or subsequent experiences, but because it could have changed relations between CD and me and some future actions of his.

No such flash ever happened between us again, although for a time I saw no less of CD, although I stayed overnight in his apartment once in a while.

5

I didn't recall them that night, or the morning after, but two previous incidents fell into a sort of line with that night.

A friend of CD's, who had become a friend of mine,

was an Irish actor named Christopher Larne, a short, warm, tubby, shiny-cheeked man in his late fifties who occasionally made gratis guest appearances with the company between his professional engagements — he was famous as Nick Bottom and the First Gravedigger — just because he loved to play Shakespeare. The summer before the Boris Kraft evening, CD had made his first trip to Europe, to England only. (He would not go to the continent for some reason he invented, but the real reason was that he spoke no foreign language and didn't want to be at a disadvantage. CD knew how to cite shortcomings as if they were proof of merit.) When he came back, he brought me a Sheffield penknife and an Edmund Kean playbill. He also said he had something to tell me.

In his theatergoing in London and in Stratford, he said, he had met some old actors who had known Chris Larne in his London days, after Ireland, before America, and they had told him that Larne, in those days at least, was homosexual. Larne now lived in Greenwich Village with a young American actor, where I had sometimes visited him, but I had always taken this arrangement as an instance of old-fashioned "bach-ing together."

I told CD that I didn't believe it of Chris. CD said that he admired my response and wanted to agree with me, but, he added sadly, he had heard the story more than once from what he called "good men." Anyway, he said, I must keep the matter to myself and, true or not, must not hold it against Chris. I didn't quite understand why he had told me the story if he didn't want my attitude toward Chris to change, except perhaps that he meant the confidence as a mark of friendship, another present he had brought me from abroad.

The other incident took place several months before the Boris Kraft evening. One morning I arrived at school to hear smudged and scurrying talk about some trouble the previous night, after rehearsal, after I had gone home. The talk that day involved Kenneth D., who taught acting in the school and was a member of the company. Among other roles, he played Orlando, and besides our relation as teacher and student, we had become friends since I was Adam.

That afternoon I had to see CD about something, and I waited in his secretary's office until he was free. At last I was admitted to the inner office. He sat staring out the window, his overcoat draped over his shoulders, a cigarette between his teeth. I said that he looked tired. He said he hadn't been to bed all night. About one o'clock in the morning, just as he had been about to undress, he had been visited by Harry O. Harry was a wealthy student who did walk-ons with the company, not a very serious fellow but, because of his money and his nonseriousness, a relief to us all from one another. Harry had told CD that, after the rehearsal, he had invited Kenneth, also his teacher, to his apartment south of Washington Square for a drink. After several drinks Kenneth had made a homosexual advance. Harry, upset but not frightened, had eased Kenneth out of the apartment and had thought he ought to tell CD right away and not over the telephone. CD had thanked Harry for coming, then had rung Kenneth who was desolate, almost suicidal. CD had gone over to Kenneth's tiny West Village apartment at 2 A.M.

"I saw the sun come up this morning," sighed CD. "We talked it out, quite calmly. Kenneth thinks the best thing is for him to get away. Right away. Not even come back to empty out his desk. I have to confess it's what I hoped he'd say. So I agreed with him." He shot an almost angry glance at me. "Don't you agree?"

"Of course," I said, out of the wealth of my experience,

flattered that my opinion had been asked and that the rest of the school was buzzing in ignorance.

"I said that I'd take care of everything for him," CD went on. "Take his classes myself for the rest of the term. Switch casts in the company where we need to, rehearse them. And as far as anyone outside will ever know, he has suddenly been taken ill."

Outside. That meant I was inside. "Of course," I said. As with the Chris Larne incident, I took the confidence as a mark of favor, but this time I related it to the company. I was a prime mover for the outward growth of the company; so CD felt, I decided, that I ought to have a private word about why a member had suddenly left. Thus, as I worked it out, this privacy about Kenneth was a confirmation of my own future.

I heard much later that, at CD's urging, Kenneth had married an extremely plain evening student from Long Island and had gone to live in her town. I don't know whether this was true: by the time I heard it, I was no longer close enough to CD to ask. Still, even then, it seemed to prove CD's concern for a friend's well-being. And at the time of Kenneth's swift exit, I thought that CD had moved promptly with handclasp and support, not with censure, to help a member of his faculty and a member of his company. I thought it was Roman.

6

The summer after graduation I scraped together enough money to go upstate for a couple of weeks and visit CD. He spent his summers in a cottage that he rented on a lake near his birthplace, only forty miles or so past the mountains where I had worked on farms in the summers of my boyhood. It had been an additional link between us that I could exchange local references with him and that I could — sometimes did — speak in the local accent without mockery.

At the beginning of the summer I sold three one-act plays in a clump. I had begun to write plays in college and had soon begun to sell them to play publishers. I had even written a long play whose rights I made over to the company, at my insistence, in a formal document; CD had given it a couple of performances, then had taken it off "for seasoning," he said, and for possible later revival. Most of my plays were short. I poured them out quickly, some of them in an hour or so between classes. I wrote so many — three dozen or so before I tired of the formula manufacture — that I had to put a pen name to some of them. I used the name of a well-known eighteenth-century actor, as an inside joke. Today some library catalogues note that this actor wrote a few short plays published in the 1930s.

Every previous summer of my college years I had been separated from CD for three months, and we had exchanged a few long letters. Now I meant to use my little windfall to see him for a couple of weeks. I wrote to ask whether he would mind my being around for a bit. If not, would he find a boarding house for me within walking distance of his cottage? He replied that he would enjoy my visit, that he would ask me to stay with him but he had married friends in his spare room, and that he would find a place for me nearby. I went up on the bus: he met me at the crossroads stop in his red convertible and drove me to a big old house about half a mile from his cottage. It was the house on the place that later became The Palace Wood.

That fact holds some facts. He took the first step, and most of the other steps, toward making it The Palace Wood, but if I hadn't gone up to visit him, he would likely never have been in the house, would possibly have dallied long about making the move he made, would possibly never have made it. The fact that it was I, of all the company members, who had gone there had something to do with his getting the idea. One of the ways he admired me — at that time — was as a goad, speaking and silent. For a time, I think, he wanted the push that my presence gave him whether I was actually talking about the company's move or not.

I had begun to itch even more about the company, now that I was out of college. CD had never explicitly promised to move out of the university, which would have meant giving up his job of course, but he knew that I believed it would happen at some reasonable time after I graduated. I said in my letter that one of the reasons I wanted to come up and visit was to talk a little about that. I was quite willing, and he knew it, to spend the rest of my life at odd little money-making jobs if I had to, to write whatever I could to make some money, so that I could be with the company. I never said that he owed me a move toward a full-time theater. But he knew what I hoped; and he hadn't discouraged it.

I walked over to his cottage the next day and splashed off his dock with him and his married friends and the husband's young brother, who were all staying there. The day after, CD drove over to see me at my much grander boarding house. A driveway ran up from the lake road beside the big lawn, then past the side of the house, then made a big loop behind the house — you could drive to the kitchen door and out without reversing. Back of that loop was a back lawn, then a grassy knoll. One side of the knoll sloped down to the edge of a bank overlooking the brook that ran out to the lake. CD said later that the moment he looked at that knoll he saw *A Midsummer Night's Dream* on it. That's what came about eventually. And where the ground leveled off on the brook side of the knoll, right on the edge of the bank, a theater was built.

The house itself was big, a huge kitchen and dining room, a big living room with a big fireplace, two upper floors with bathrooms on each floor, plenty of space for members of the company. However, right from the beginning, CD planned separate quarters for himself, on the upper floor of the theater building along with the dressing rooms.

Before the end of my two weeks at the lake, he broached the subject to me. He wanted to buy this place and build a theater behind it. He wanted to do indoor and outdoor performances, in the theater and on the knoll.

It was a move, though it was far from the move I had been hoping for. This place would be used in summer only, of course, when the lake people were here. For the rest of the year the company would work as before in New York, at the university theaters. But, CD said, this meant that the company could have the whole year, instead of three-quarters. Many of us would be able to stay up there, the rest would be able to make extended visits and perform as they could. Work, more intensive study and training, could press on when we were together all day all summer.

75

A bit disappointed, I was enthusiastic. What he said was true, but I had been hoping for more. I restrained the disappointment and spoke the enthusiasm. I could see that this move kept CD safe for a while at the university, along with the others who taught there and elsewhere. But at least this project was a partial pledge to the future. And at least it would rid me of that three-month summer gap that I hated.

CD especially liked the idea because this was his home country — not so far from what I thought of as partly my own — and because the theater could be built by his brother-in-law, the carpenter who lived twenty miles up the valley.

Cy Wheeler was his name, and this man who was to build our theater looked as if he had stepped out of a nineteenth-century Yankee play — lean, turkey-necked, big Adam's apple, small blue twinkling eyes behind rimless glasses, the outsize hands of a man who has been doing manual labor all his life. I saw a lot of Mr. Wheeler in the next few years, worked a little with him (as did other men in the company) in the last weeks of finishing up, and never spent time with him without hearing some wry country anecdote or aphorism, usually flat but endearing. Sometimes a situation would draw from him a line of the Bible, usually misquoted. I liked him because he was the kind of countryman I had worshipped as a boy and because he told me stories of CD as a boy — he and CD's sister were much older. "Didn't surprise me a bit when he said he was 'bout to build this place for his boys." The women of the company never really registered with Mr. Wheeler. "Allus liked a bunch of boys 'round him, baseball team 'r this here colony." Mr. Wheeler never called it a theater, always an artists' colony. The local people always referred to The Palace Wood as the colony.

He told me stories of how hard CD had worked at his studies in high school to get a scholarship, and at jobs, to get himself to college. At the time CD was doing it, before the First War, it was something of a rarity for boys of his economic level, in this part of the world, to go to college. CD was an orphan, living with his sister and Mr. Wheeler, and he was "jes' plain set on gettin' to that college." I felt as if I was getting a glimpse behind the scenes.

The future Palace Wood was easy to buy — one of the things that had encouraged CD was the fact that the owner was looking to sell. The theater, which was only a one-layer wooden shell, uninsulated, with one steel I-beam to hold the roof, was put up in a couple of years, as Mr. Wheeler could find time to work on it and CD could find money for expenses. After he had used as much of his savings as he wanted to, CD took a mortgage to pay bills, in the belief that the company's earnings would repay him. Those earnings, up there and in New York, could not have helped much: most of the comany income went to keep the place running. I'm sure that CD never got repaid until he sold the place years later.

I helped, too, as I could. One day CD asked me to write a children's play for the company. "These people keep asking whether we have anything for children. Some of your poems aren't bad. I thought you might just be able to do it. Something in the fairy tale vein. A lot of songs. I think you'd better try it." I scoured fairy tale collections, pieced together a story that could be played in costumes we had already, wrote it in rhymed verse, and Mr. Wheeler's daughter, a piano teacher, composed music for the lyrics I sent her. It all went well. When we did guest performances of Shakespeare in the metropolitan area, at suburban high schools usually, we would throw in a 4 P.M. performance of my one-hour play for an extra fee. When the children laughed and screamed and applauded, I felt imperial; and I felt even more soundly married to a goal.

7

During the time when the theater was being built, we all got an extra chance to contribute. A man in Albany made a deal with a college nearby to bring us up for a special new production in an old Albany theater, to raise funds for that college, for us, and of course for himself. The company had some reputation by then among schools and colleges in the state, and the story of The Palace Wood, the fact that it was under construction, had made a small stir in upstate newspapers, including those in Albany, which was within comfortable driving distance of the lake.

The play they wanted in Albany was *Julius Caesar*. CD welcomed the guaranteed fee for The Wood and thought it would be a good idea anyway to add *Caesar* to the repertory. The play would be very salable to schools, and anyway we had more men than women in the company. He accepted, to perform in Albany for a week around Easter. Those of us who taught would be on holiday, and those of us in other jobs would have some reason to ask for time off.

CD studied the Variorum edition of *Caesar* and old promptbooks that he had collected or copied, including one left to him by his mentor, who had been in Beerbohm Tree's production. That was CD's usual method of preparation: to learn as much as he could about what had been done with the text in the theater, to choose, revise, and build on what had been done. It gave me the feeling of picking up a torch and freshening it.

He appointed me stage manager for *Caesar*. He explained his general ideas of staging, and I designed the one set. This sounds more accomplished than it was. There were the usual black drapes: the setting was a wide carpeted flight of three shallow steps that cut across the stage diagonally from back center to the down left corner, with a broad platform at the top leading off upstage left. It was simple and useful, with good lighting. I did the lighting. I was the Soothsayer and a member of the mob in the funeral oration scene.

We had often played dates in the vicinity of New York, but we had never made an overnight trip. We had never really toured. This trip was to be for a week.

Albany! The word was magic, especially since I would see the place as an actor on my first visit, a member of a company, the company. And we were going to play in a famous old touring theater, fallen mostly into disuse even then but full of history. (The last time I was there it was a bowling alley.)

We arrived in Albany the night before we were to open. We stayed in an old hotel, now gone, which had the oldest waiter I had ever seen. After eleven, when we came back from a film, he served us rarebits kept warm by small metal eggs. These eggs, two halves that screwed together, were filled with hot water, then were submerged in the rarebits. The waiter said he had brought those eggs with him from England fifty years before and didn't know whether they could be replaced.

Early next morning at the theater we built the steps and

hung the lights and drapes. We always did all the work ourselves. When we played in places that had stagehands, like this theater, the job of the stage manager — myself, in this case — was to persuade the stagehands to let us do the work ourselves, that we wouldn't interfere with their salaries. The women in the company took care of costumes and props.

We needed a bier for Caesar's body. At rehearsals in New York we had mocked up something for the four attendants to carry. Our Albany entrepreneur, who had come down to see the final rehearsals, had told us not to bother about bringing a bier. He would arrange to borrow one from an Albany undertaker.

He didn't. I learned this at noon of the opening day. I had to find one quickly. I telephoned several undertakers who either didn't know what I was talking about — a four-handed body-carrier that would rest on the ground on four short legs — or else said biers just weren't used any more. At last, when I was ready to rush to a lumberyard for supplies to build one, an undertaker said on the phone that he thought he had one somewhere.

I hurried over in a taxi. By the time I got there he seemed to have forgotten my call; then he said, "Oh, yes, that old thing. Come this way." He opened a door in the back of his showroom and strolled jauntily ahead. I followed eagerly. It was fairly dark in there, and it was only after I was halfway down the long room that I realized I was striding past corpses on tables on either side, in various stages of embalming and costuming. The air was thickly chemical.

In a shed behind his workroom he found it, exactly what was needed, dirty but sound. We wiped it off, then he helped me to carry it to the front, past the departed. I had a strange angelic feeling, carrying something to light and life out of this room of the dead.

Outside I told him how grateful we were and that I would be sure to return it at the end of the week. I gave him a pair of tickets. He looked at them as if they themselves were supposed to be objects of entertainment and were not entertaining him. "Swell," he said, putting them away. "Now how are you going to get this thing to your theater?"

In my desperation I hadn't really considered the problem. I had assumed I'd get a taxi.

"Never," he said. "They'll never take you." He opened the workroom door and called, "Tim." A smocked man appeared from somewhere wearing rubber gloves and with slimy tubes in his hand. The boss said, "Give this fellow a hand with this old thing, will yez? He needs to get it over to the theater."

Tim stowed his tubes and gloves, and he and I shoved the bier inside a hearse. But the other undertakers had been right — these things weren't used any more. The bier handles stuck out six inches past the end of the hearse: the back door wouldn't close. We couldn't drive with the back door swinging, so I had to sit in the rear of the hearse on the bier, holding a cord attached to the back door to keep it steady. We drove about twelve blocks through crowded streets, clearly raising questions in the minds of passersby.

I loved it. This was trouping.

That night I raised some other questions in the audience. The performance went well until the funeral scene. (The bier, covered with a purple cloth, looked splendid.) Everyone who could be spared — about ten of us plus a few Albany recruits — had been pressed into the funeral mob. CD had asked me to keep the mob in dim light because there were so few and because what we wanted was the sense of a group, rather than individuals. When I finished my Soothsayer in the Senate scene, all this between running the lights and cuing the music, I ripped off my cowl and long gown and wispy beard and slipped into a short tunic — too short, but the mob was in the dark anyway.

We in the mob had been rehearsed to run out downstage right, away from the platform, after Mark Antony had incited us. Then Antony spoke his last two lines, then the curtain closed for the act break. The curtain rope in this Albany theater was downstage left. Only one man in the company was available at that moment to be downstage left and work the curtain — our Cassius. All the rest of us were in the mob, exiting on the opposite side. Cassius had to go up to his dressing room after the Senate scene, change into his armor for the tent scene, and get back to downstage left in time to pull the curtain at the end of the funeral scene. That afternoon we hadn't rehearsed a stagehand on the curtain because all of them looked so feeble that I wasn't sure any of them would live until evening and because the stage manager (myself) was on stage at the moment and couldn't cue the stagehand. He certainly couldn't be left to time the curtain on his own. Our Cassius had tried it all out at the run-through, with costume change, and it had worked fine.

Antony, in the column of golden light on the platform at left, grew toward the finish of his speech. We Romans got heated. Antony drew back the purple on the bier and showed us the wounds on the body of Caesar (CD). We Romans got more heated. Then Antony finished in a blaze, and we Romans ran off downstage right, shouting

"Revenge! Revenge!" We got off, then I heard Antony speak his two quietly gloating lines, then I expected to hear the curtain close. Nothing. I fought through the mob, back to the downstage right corner. The curtain was open. The downstage left corner was empty. No Cassius.

Antony was standing in his golden light above Caesar's bier, his hand still upraised. I could see a flicker of question cross his strong face. The stage seemed immense, never quieter. A frozen continent.

I ran across that endless stage, shouting "Revenge! Revenge!" all alone, ran through the bright light with my too-short tunic bobbing. I thought I saw Antony's eyes widen. I thought I saw dead Caesar twitch. After an hour or so, I got to the curtain rope and pulled it as if I were saving lives.

Cassius, it seemed, had got jammed in an old toilet whose door had stuck. Well, perhaps there were a few people in the audience who thought it a neat touch to characterize one of the mob individually — as an exhibitionist, obviously, but one who had a mind of his own and meant to wreak vengeance for Caesar's murder in his own single-handed way.

8

The summer that The Palace Wood was to open, the company arrived there at the end of June. CD asked a few of us, me and four other men, to go up with him early in June to get the place ready. I was glad I had no job to hamper me. He and two of the others were on their summer holiday from teaching; the other two, like myself, had work they could quit and go back to as they chose.

How big the moment seemed. It impresses me still, when I think what it would take these days in heaving and tugging of lives, in foundation grants, to get such a project going. How easy it seemed then, how natural.

We hired a truckman from a town near The Wood to come down to New York. We loaded his open truck with company stuff — racks of costumes, drapes, lights, witches' cauldron, and all the rest — and covered it all with a tarpaulin. Two men got in the cab with the driver. Another man and I chained the tailgate to horizontal, tied Hamlet's chair and Macbeth's throne on it, and he and I rode up sitting on them. We were lashed in, and I had a string attached to my waist that ran around to the driver's arm so that I could signal in case anything went wrong.

Nothing went wrong. The world poured away behind us as we rode up to our theater.

I hadn't been back to the lake since I had boarded there, but I had heard from CD, and from others whom he'd invited to accompany him, how work was progressing. He had chosen the name. I had wanted to call it Bankside, both for the Elizabethan reference and because the place was close to two banks, the brook and the lake into which it flowed. CD liked Bankside, but The Palace Wood was the name he had thought of. When the truck drove in and around to the back and I saw the theater standing there, not yet painted but all built, I was chill with excitement. Then I thought calmly: "This is what happens next in my life." And then I felt gratitude. This meant the end of the three-month vacancies in my life. From now on I was enclosed.

We took possession, the five of us and CD in his green

sweater, in the brisk first week of June. All of us except CD were moored to the place because he had the only car, but nobody cared. We fell to work, preparing for the arrival of the others and the beginning of our first Wood season, a month off. While CD was busy, mostly with banks and newspapers and printers and suppliers, the five of us worked in the house and, under Mr. Wheeler's direction, on the theater. Then we hung the lights and drapes and travelers. I had often bragged of my summers on farms forty miles south, so in teasing reward CD put the lawn mowing in my charge. There was a lot of it. We had only an old hand-mower, there were big lawns front and back and a steep incline on one side of the house. It was very hard work, but I liked not complaining about it and getting it done.

It gave CD another straight-faced way of dealing with my jokes. If the others at the round table laughed or did not laugh at a pun, CD, stonily, would look out over the lawn and say, "Grass seems to be getting a bit ahead of you."

And, recognizing my Germanic instinct for order, he asked me to draft the House Rules. They were his rules, of course, but I enjoyed phrasing them and even added some for his approval. He didn't want slacks on women (culottes were permitted), he didn't want leather heels on anyone (floors were uncarpeted), everyone up by 7:30, no visiting in rooms without permission of all occupants (each room had at least two men or two women), no cars without permission of the director (which meant no cars). Transportation and laundering were to be provided by the individual, room and meals by the company (the only compensation any of us ever received). The members were to share dishwashing and table-waiting and house-

85

keeping. Meals would be prepared by the woman who also made our costumes; the kitchen was her domain. There were twenty-nine rules. I still have a crumbling copy.

During that first June, all six of us had our meals, weather permitting, on the front porch of the house, sitting at the round table that was also Sir Toby's in the tavern scene of *Twelfth Night.* Sunny or gray, warm or nippy, any weather but driving rain or wind, we had our meals outdoors, with the lawn lolling down to the lake road. At breakfast I was so hungry or excited or both that I habitually overloaded my toast with jam; it was messy, and I was clucked over. I even liked that, I liked the situation that made it possible.

The curious, contradictory fact remained that, as excited as I was, as much as I felt that I needed the company and that I was useful to it, I knew even more clearly that CD really didn't like me. Something else was happening: though I admired his mind and manner and in many ways lived by his word, I saw more clearly where his virtues ended. In my reading I had become more interested in writers whom he disliked, writers hardly new in the world even then, Ibsen and Joyce and Faulkner and Eliot. In the theater I had begun to think that not every innovation was arbitrarily corruptive. Deepest of all differences between us was politics. It was a stormy time, the blackness of the Depression had been only somewhat brightened by the New Deal, which I welcomed but thought skimpy, and communism and fascism were in everybody's mind and mouth. CD was a country conservative. He hated Roosevelt. He didn't understand why an owner didn't sheerly own, why a dissatisfied employee didn't just move on. Although he called the rising Hitler a son of a bitch, he added sorrowfully, as did many in those days, that in honesty you had to admit that the Jews had brought a lot of it on themselves. He never wanted to understand that there are differences between communism and socialism and got irritated when I tried to explain. "If that sort of thing interests you so much, brother, maybe you're in the wrong outfit." The word "brother" from him was always a warning.

And it froze me. I was dependent on the company morally and, in the truest sense, vocationally. I didn't want to be excommunicated. I was miserable much of the time: because I hated being poor, especially because it made me borrow from or sponge off girls; because CD withdrew to a height at least as often as he came close to me, my teacher-friend; because very few of the people I knew recognized me as a superior person; because there was more frustration than satisfaction in almost every moment of my life. But — this was the paradox and redemption — all this misery was contained. It all existed within the happiness of being in the company. My life, whatever its pains and tormenting itches, was on a road, ascendant, and I didn't want to be shunted off that road.

This was true even though I could perceive the company and the world well enough, the company and my mind outside it. Some of the members were surely not distinguished, as people or as actors, but in combination, the work was reputable, particularly because three or four of them were truly fine, most were committed, and CD gave it a consistent spirit. We were pointed, I could see, toward restoration, toward revitalizing a theater that had once been, rather than building a classical theater in any kind of accord with the present or future, but the restoration wasn't musty, it had blood in it. Our work was, I'm sure, lumpy and bumpy, but it was not precious. If CD couldn't see what was good about Gielgud's Hamlet, because it was modern in temper, at least he helped our Hamlet to full, beautiful, traditional performance. At its best the company was as reliable as the most reliable work of 1890 (I would guess), which is about what we wanted even if we never thought of it that way.

I still dream of some of those performances, some of the lovely lost moments. And I still have nightmares about mixing up spotlight plugs or forgetting lines. A few of my dreams are in the theaters down on Washington Square, but most are up at The Palace Wood, in the new theater or the performances on the knoll next to it. Most of the dreams and the nightmares are about that place.

9

June ended, the others arrived, rehearsals began. So did classes. That was another way we were to use these summers, classes that were taught by those who had knowledges to share. One of our men, Alexis, was a gymnast and fencer, so every day there was a session of exercise for all and a session of fencing for the men. Some of us had taken theater fencing in school; we polished it here. Alexis had a young cousin who had originally been brought in to be the Indian boy in the *Dream* and was now a ballet student progressing rapidly. CD, who liked him and kept him about a good deal, had invited him up for the summer. This boy, about sixteen that summer, commanded us all out on the back lawn every morning in ballet exercises and simple combinations. One woman in the company, by vocation a high-school teacher, had been studying singing for years with a famous coach. Here at The Wood she gave us vocal lessons three times a week, less for singing than for voice placement and control. She taught us solfeggio. We all did singing exercises and tried to hear pitch.

And we had meetings with CD. We talked about policy and theory, not of our plans — he never consulted with anyone on what plays we were to do or how they were to be cast or anything of that sort. But we did talk about the company as a body, and why we wanted to be in it. On the inside cover of my copy of Frank Damrosch's *Popular Method of Sightsinging,* the book we used in our singing class, are the penciled notes I made at one of those meetings. The heading is Company Principles. First, there are six sheerly theatrical points, from permanent membership to re-production — the idea of adding a play to the repertory and always keeping it fresh enough to do it again relatively quickly. Then there are six qualifications for membership: idealism, integrity, enthusiasm, endurance, humanity, and versatility. Each of these has two subdivisions. For instance, under idealism are: a) vision; b) humility. Then there are three overall aims: personal development, realization of these company principles, establishment of a complete theater for these things and a school to carry them on.

I still read those notes once in a while, equally without irony or glow.

Looking back, I can see that what we had, during the summers at The Wood, was what would now be called a commune, except that there was no unconventionality of morals — as policy, anyway. We would not have wanted it and CD would not have tolerated it. Democracy was total until it reached CD. He would have loathed the communes that later came about, but he understood the spiritual power of community, of common purpose, and he made something of it.

I mowed. I stage-managed. I played small parts. I took my turn on dishwashing and table-waiting crews. I did some barbering of men's hair — we wore it long for Shakespeare, years before long hair was fashionable for men, and it wasn't difficult to trim. I handled the music for shows and worked on the lighting, indoors and out. I occasionally did a spell in the box office. Once a week I went to the neighboring towns with our housekeeper on her shopping trip. Since she was also our costume-maker, she was always busy for at least a couple of hours in various stores, getting food and sewing goods. While this was going on, I walked around with posters for our theater, asking shopkeepers to let me put them in windows. These people were used to getting passes from movie houses and circuses in return for this favor, but CD didn't believe in passes, possibly just because others gave them. This meant I had to do special pleading with the shop people, embarrassed, emboldened by embarrassment. Often it worked.

That first summer our business began well. It continued almost as well in following summers. Every season we ran into some resistance because only a small part of our repertory was like other summer-theater fare. Most of our plays were Shakespeare. In different seasons we also did one Sheridan, one Goldsmith, one Barrie, and several Shaw. CD bowed far enough to do, one summer, a bill of Noel Coward short plays and, another summer, a parody 1890s melodrama. The white-jacketed and flower-frocked types in the audience were not always happy, but there wasn't much alternative entertainment around and they liked coming to the place itself, particularly when we played outdoors on the knoll with lawn chairs and benches stretched across the grass. We built up a following that came fifty or sixty miles to see us, as far as from Albany, a group of faithful who followed various actors from role to role through the seasons.

Even the faithful, however, sometimes objected in person or by letter to some of the casting, almost always of women. CD brushed off all such objections as philistine. If he cast, as Lady Macbeth, a genteel spinsterish college teacher who was intelligent but rather remote or, as the child Margaret in *Dear Brutus,* a woman of thirty-eight whose chief asset was that she was short, the audience's job was to take his decisions as writ, to sympathize with our difficulties and objectives.

His big casting mistakes, until his last mistake, were always with women.

Still, that first season and the seasons after, we had at least half a house at our shows, and sometimes — on Saturday nights — a full house. So we got along. Whatever their feelings about any one production, people were impressed with our scope and seriousness. We had an air — amazing to me now but not at all then — of complete ease in such a large purpose: to become a permanent theater of some quality. We simply assumed, without public manifesto or appeal, that this was what to do. We simply did it, faults and all; and if CD was responsible for almost all the faults, he was also responsible for the simple assumption of purpose.

Faults and all, I wanted nothing more than to live in the company. By the time I was twenty-four, in 1940, five years after I had graduated from college, I had never really worked anywhere else and never really expected to work anywhere else.

10

Out of the drama school toward the end of the 1930s came Nicholas K., of Greek parentage, tall, slightly bow-legged, not especially good-looking except for very black eyes and curly black hair. CD had taken great interest in him as a student. Before long, Nicholas was invited to do walk-ons with the company and to play small parts. Before much longer, he was invited to become a member. It was more or less what had happened to me eight or nine years before; this was the first time it had happened so quickly since then. And I had never been made as close a companion as Nicholas was. He was very often with CD, was often — which made me particularly jealous — taken to dinner by CD at the Players Club, to which I had never been asked.

Not long after he became a member of the company, Nicholas was put into leading roles, into Hamlet and Romeo and Petruchio. CD's official line at the start was that this extremely talented boy would help to exercise the very principle of repertory by alternating those roles with David B., who had been playing them. Some of us couldn't see the talent in Nicholas, though none of us said so. There was no way to say so: the idea of saying anything about it, to CD, was not part of our being.

Within a year the plan of alternation was quite forgotten: those roles and other large ones belonged to Nicholas. Sweet and greatly gifted David, in every way superior to Nicholas, was so dedicated to the company that he took on Bernardo and Tybalt and Hortensio as if this subordination was good for his soul, as if he was glad to be tested. I think now that it was this misuse of David — when he was finally able to admit it to himself as misuse, as betrayal of devotion — that first cracked his being. The cracks were later deepened by four stultifying years of army life during the war that ruined a possibly great actor.

At the time I defended CD's actions to outsiders who were critical and to members who cocked eyebrows. I had to subscribe or change my life, and I did not yet want to change.

The winter seasons in the city became even more settled at the two university theaters after The Palace Wood opened. From time to time CD now began to speak of long-range plans for those theaters, of even closer connection between the company and the university — possibly the company as a teaching component of the school. Gradually it became clear that The Wood was not a first step toward independence. The Wood gave CD an "outside" theater without forcing him to leave his university snuggery.

In one part of my mind I began to think of ways to adjust to that kind of future, because what I saw in the theater outside seemed so much less. But in my secretest mind I began to feel panic. I was in my mid twenties. Was the company still worth my life?

At rehearsals CD behaved to the rest of us as before, warmly or coldly. But he watched Nicholas with wonder, sometimes even listened to him with his eyes closed. Afterward he would very nearly express gratitude to him,

93

sometimes tentatively offer a suggestion to make Nicholas's performance even more "pure poetry." Nicholas was not vain about all this, he merely took it seriously. Even if I had thought him extremely talented, CD's behavior toward him would have been disquieting. And I couldn't begin to agree with CD's opinion of him — by the standards that CD himself had taught me.

Now he and Nicholas were almost always together outside rehearsals. They consumed a lot of Scotch together and joked about the rows of empties along the penthouse wall. CD invited other people to the apartment less and less, me hardly ever. He gave Nicholas a carnelian signet ring, identical to the one he wore. He kept taking Nicholas to the Players. I knew, even then, that my feelings about these things were childish, but I had been almost a child when I met CD and had spent nearly ten years in a relation based on that beginning.

Sometimes a remembrance of that Boris Kraft evening crossed my mind, with tandem thoughts of Chris Larne and Kenneth. There were plenty of sly remarks from others about CD and Nicholas, but I always waved them off: only a mean mind could not accept the possibility of friendship between men without homosexuality. Once CD took me aside to tell me that a woman we knew, who had tried to get into the company and had failed, had made a slurring remark to him of "a most serious kind," and he got so angrily white that I was willing to take the anger as intended. I understood that he might have been doing an act — I saw that he might have been doing the same thing earlier about Chris Larne and Kenneth — but I wanted the act to succeed still.

That conversation, in his office, was one of the few I had alone with him in that last year.

Every time I looked outside the company, things

seemed more and more like a jungle, and yet I began to hate myself a little for seeing no way. Because every time I looked inside these days, I had to judge the company by the means that CD himself had taught me, by all that had brought me here in the first place.

It had to end, and it ended. Sometime in the winter of 1939 Mr. J. became interested in the company. Mr. J. had a daughter in the school who had done bits with the company and some dancing in such plays as the *Dream*. Mr. J. also had several million dollars. (He later acquired many millions and became a famous patron.) He liked to put money into art, and the company appealed to him. He liked CD, he liked me, especially because of my children's play, he liked some other members whom he had met. He was awestruck with our work and our record. If he had any reservations about us, which I never heard, they were outweighed by his love of idealism. I felt that Mr. J. wanted to use us the way a marauding medieval baron used a chaplain to do his praying for him: we were to do Mr. J.'s idealism for him.

I was afraid that he had arrived a couple of years too late, but I hoped that he might be able to recharge CD about moving out just by putting the means so easily to hand. Mr. J., stocky, ebullient, and hoarse, invited CD to dinner several times at his Westchester home late in 1939 and early in 1940. CD reported to some of us on those evenings, taking care to make pleasant amused remarks about the lavish furnishings, lavish food, and lavish Mrs. J. After three or four of those dinners, CD told us that Mr. J. himself had raised the subject of backing us, of finding us a place outside the university, of endowing us well enough so that at the beginning we could pay ourselves a little until we got established.

CD's voice, when he told us this, had a tone I knew well:

careful noncommitment. Nicholas was sitting next to him. I asked CD — almost numbly, because I could hardly believe what I had heard — whether, if it happened, this would mean his leaving the university. He answered as if an idiot had asked. "If it comes about, severance from the university would follow, I assume." He ended with a glance at Nicholas, who snickered.

Not long afterward, an Italian restaurant on Bleecker Street announced that it was going to close. It was an old place that occupied a whole small building. I heard that Mr. J. had talked to the owners about the possibility of buying the building and converting it into a theater for us. (It's now a film theater.)

This was in the late spring of 1940. That summer, toward the end of July, Mr. J. came up for his first visit to The Palace Wood. It was tacitly understood that he would then make his decisions. He didn't go to a luxe summer hotel in the nearest town. In order to get more of the feeling of our place, to be able to saunter in and out, he took a room at the boarding house just down the road from The Wood where our one married couple also boarded. (The husband, Tim C., was not an actor. He was a high-school teacher who spent summers up there with his wife, a member of the company.) Mr. J. had most of his meals with us, usually at CD's corner table, and he circulated frequently to the other tables in the big sunny dining room. A starry-eyed rapture shone in this man who, I'm sure, was generally tough.

The day before he was supposed to leave, he left. With his daughter. I didn't see his big Cadillac drive off, I just noticed at lunchtime that it was gone. For a drive, I assumed. But he didn't come back.

I ran into my closest friend going over to the theater

for rehearsal in midafternoon, and I asked him where Mr. J. was. I expected him to say something about an excursion with the daughter. My friend gave me a quick small headshake which meant he couldn't talk about it just then in front of the others. Later he told me what he had heard from Tim, the husband of our actress in the boarding house. Mr. J. had told Tim that he had been wandering through the theater that morning and had gone upstairs where there were dressing rooms, some doubling as bedrooms, and CD's quarters, Mr. J. had strolled down the short hall up there. The door to CD's bedroom was open. On the bed in their bathing trunks, apparently just before they left for the lake, were CD and Nicholas, lying with their arms around each other, hugging and teasing and chuckling. They hadn't seen Mr. J., who had moved on as soon as he recovered. He was sufficiently shocked to want to get away from The Wood at once. He had told Tim: "I'm through with this bunch if that kind of man is running it."

I understood why Mr. J. was shocked, but I wished I could have explained to him. CD often embraced men in the company, kissed them on the cheek after long separation, often slept with them, in the literal sense. He used to joke about one man in particular, now married and still an occasional visitor, whose big behind had kept him warm on cold nights. I didn't want Mr. J. to draw sexual inferences, I didn't want to draw them myself. I wanted to explain that what he had seen was only uninhibited, large-spirited male companionship.

CD soon heard what Mr. J. had said. He spoke to some of us after the performance that night. He wasn't whitely angry, he just dismissed the whole incident as low-minded misinterpretation by a gross vulgarian. He treated Mr. J.'s sudden exit, from The Wood and from our prospects, as if, at the last moment, a philistine had been frightened off by principle, by high-minded unconventionality, by the lack of foreseeable profit; and he gave the story an edge to imply that the trouble, finally, lay in the fact that Mr. J. was Jewish. ("I'm quite sure those friends of his in Purchase will tell him he was foolish to get mixed up with a mad gentile idealist in the first place.") Handled this way, Mr. J.'s disappearance was just what CD needed to prove that the outside world was not quite good enough for him, for the company. The move outward had been stopped, and it was someone else who had stopped it. Once again, CD was right.

I sat alone in one of the lawn chairs that night, for a long while. When I got up to go to bed, something struck me, a thought struck me almost like a blow on the forehead. Perhaps CD had deliberately left the door of his room open. He knew that Mr. J. was around. From his window he could easily have seen Mr. J. walking across the lawn toward the theater. Matters had been progressing with Mr. J., Bleecker Street was becoming possible. And CD knew something of Mr. J.'s propriety.

I didn't go to bed. I walked up the lake road to the nearest village — three miles — and back. The moon was full. I felt pieces of myself slipping off me as I walked. By the time I got back I felt skinned.

Of course I had to find another life. I knew that I had known that, now I admitted to myself that I knew it. Whatever it was like outside, I couldn't spend the rest of my life as a supporter of something increasingly chipped, as a lackey of CD's romance with Nicholas. I didn't know whether it was sexual — I still don't know whether CD was homosexual in practice — but I could see now that this was the least important part of it.

What had once seemed a strong wonderful fight to pre-serve tradition, to revitalize it, now seemed a deer park for CD and his romance. Apart from everything else, I was sick that the health of the past, whatever was healthy in it, had been struck such a blow by the man who had taught me to want it.

Through the summer, others began to feel the same. David B. began to be cynical. The company, though it was still together, became porous.

I stayed through the next season in the city because I cared about a girl in the school — no longer Enid — who would not graduate until June. CD knew about us, and I didn't want to compromise her in the school. But he smelled that I was disaffected. He was shrewd as ever in many ways, even brilliant. He must have known how his treatment of Nicholas would affect me in time, he must fundamentally have wanted it to alter me. I don't know how he felt about alienating some of the others, which he was also doing, but I could only be a nagging reminder of an earlier plan. I could only be a hair shirt. No word was said. Because of what had been, he would never have ex-plicitly urged me to leave: there was too much Roman left in him for that. But I thought we both knew it was just a matter of time.

He sealed my decision by producing my play. It was the play that he had produced a few years before and had put away for "seasoning." For a while I had asked about it. He had either replied amiably that the time wasn't right for the company just then or replied brusquely that if I didn't want to leave the matter to him, I could have the play back. "It's up to you, brother."

I had almost forgotten about the play. Suddenly he put it on the spring schedule and asked me to do some revi-sions. I was puzzled at his decision in view of the growing freeze between us. Then one of the men told me that CD had told him, "I always pay my debts," with an expression of quittance.

Nicholas had a leading role. At rehearsals CD and he snickered at some of the lines in his part. Sometimes I had to change them on the spot; sometimes CD would change them without asking. In general he was irritated by the fact that I was the author and had to be consulted at all. It had not been like this when we had done the play before, or my play for children.

I endured it because if he wanted to pay his debts, I was going to let him. A few performances were given. They went all right, but I didn't like the play as done. Anyway, I would never have wanted to go through such an experience again, and since one 'of my ties to the company had been my hope to write for it occasionally, still another tie was cut.

In April of 1941 I got a memorandum from CD, addressed to all the members, asking us to signify our intention of being at The Wood that summer. We had never had such a request before. I thought he had asked it of all so that he could ask it of me.

I felt chopped across the chest, but I was glad that I had to declare myself. Even here I was his disciple. I wrote a short note as I felt he might have written it.

I said I would not be able to go to The Wood that summer. It was all that the memo had asked. Two lines for ten years. Ten young years. As I pulled down the mailbox lid and posted the letter, my hands seemed to be in a drawing by William Blake.

By return I got a note from CD, equally brief. He assumed that my note meant I was severing my connection with the company. It was just what I had expected, the speed, the brevity, the point. In a high inimical way, which had nothing to do with our dealings with each other, we understood each other in some degree.

I was the only one who withdrew that spring. During the rest of the spring there were a few curt nods from CD, a dignified respectful reserve from me. Then the last performance. It would have been neat if the play could have been *As You Like It* with me as Adam, but it was the *Dream* with me as Starveling, doing the lights and music. By the time the performance was over, CD had left.

Then, at twenty-five, I began an alternative life, in the present, a series of alternative lives.

11

My closest friend went up to The Wood that summer. He lasted five weeks. He had begun drama school with me in 1931 and, since 1935, had been teaching in the school. When he got back to town he told me that CD's behavior with Nicholas had become so insufferable that he had resigned from the company and from his teaching job. CD wrote to him and telephoned him, then and in the fall, but he never saw CD again.

The company faded. What was left was finished by the war. The war gave CD his excuse for the company's dissolution. People told me later that he said my conspiracies against him had weakened the company and the war had finished it.

Three years after I left, when my second novel was serialized in a magazine, CD wrote me a note. Part of the novel took place at a summer theater on a lake. CD wrote: "Some of the settings register aptly with me." I don't remember if I answered.

In the mid 1940s a theater agent who was a friend of mine told me that a young actor had been to see him, a man unknown to him who had nevertheless played a lot of Shakespearean leads with some company and was only in his early twenties. It was Nicholas. His acting career did not prosper, although he acted from time to time. I heard that he married.

CD sold The Palace Wood around 1950 and died a few years later. His heart had grown weak, I was told, and there had been several bad attacks. The last attack killed him in an ambulance on the way from his apartment to a hospital. The obituary said nothing substantial about him, nothing accurate about the company. The photograph in the newspaper had been taken at a banquet some years before. He had on his brown-rimmed eyeglasses and was wearing an old-fashioned dinner jacket. He looked askew.

When he died, I thought: What a villain he was. What a bad man. Today all of us know that there is no such thing as a villain, but each of us has his exceptions.

How much he taught me, how much that is important to me and that I could not have learned elsewhere. It was paid for.

A few years ago my friend in the company, who is still my friend, told me he had heard that The Palace Wood, the theater itself, had burned down. I thought I felt the last bond bursting. But I was wrong.

Album of Comic-Book Life

1

I BECAME A SUCCESS in December of 1942. For the previous ten months I had been an editor and staff writer for a small company that supplied comic-book pages, all lettered and ready for engraving, to a magazine publisher. We were subcontractors. Now, after less than a year in the business, I had been hired as an editor at Tappan Publications, a huge firm whose comic books, which were just one division of their line, were among the biggest in the field. My friends in the comic trade were agape. Not only had I zoomed to the top in less than a year, I wouldn't even have to write scripts any more. This was prestige — just editing. I was given three magazines at Tappan: *Major Mighty,* which was one of the big three in the country, *Nick Noonday,* which was a runner-up, and a new one they were starting. And, said my trade pals, I was still in my twenties. What would I not accomplish.

I liked their wonderment all the more because this was only the secondary part of my life, as a few of them knew. Every morning I got up at five-thirty and for a couple of hours worked on writing of my own before I went to the office. I arrived at nine or so feeling invigorated because I had got up early and had already done some of my own work. And here I was, sparkling at my Number Two job, pushing ahead of people to whom it was Number One, Number Only. I felt luxurious. I enjoyed the praise, enjoyed it doubly because I had private superiority, and I enjoyed the job, too, as one always enjoys to some degree any work that one can do well.

The earlier comic-book job, which I had taken after my first novel had been published in relative secrecy, had meant some pleasure and much drag. I liked working with the three or four old men, free-lancers, who did the hand-coloring on the "silver prints." These were small photostats of the artists' large black-and-white pages which were hand-colored as guides for the engraver. The old men were Hitler refugees, painters down on their luck. I particularly liked old Schlosser whose father had been chief prompter of the Vienna Opera for years and who had many stories about singers and conductors who were mythical to me. But I disliked having to grind out three or four five- or six-page comic scripts a week. Nowadays, when I see James Bond films with pits of alligators, with cannons concealed in hubcaps, I recognize that they are doing now what I was doing then, and see once again a dominant element in my life: bad timing.

My best pleasure in that first job had nothing to do with the job itself. I got my draft-call in April — there was a war on — and the boss hired someone to replace me. I was given a 4-F rating by the examiners because of an operation I'd had a few years before, and when I went back to tell the boss, there was someone else at my desk. Times were good, the boss was feeling flush, so he kept both me and Fred B., the new man. Fred had done some newspaper work and later went back to journalism — today he is a well-known television correspondent — but he had another talent. In the months we worked together, he taught me something about billiards during the lunch hour. A quick sandwich or a frank-and-beans pot at the Automat on Sixth Avenue, then upstairs to the billiard parlor. Not pool, which he thought vulgar and debased, but classical billiards. It was Fred who had passed on the tip about the opening at Tappan, which didn't interest him because he wanted to get back to journalism, and it meant the end of my billiard lessons when they hired me. What I remember most vividly about that earlier job — I can't remember the name of one of the magazines — is the smell of chalk and the rich way those three heavy balls rolled over the green cloth and the way they clicked — for Fred much more than for me.

My new office at Tappan was high in a high Broadway office building, a large room with a fine view and seven other desks, the entire editorial staff of the comics department. I had been hired by the editorial director of the whole company and had met the head of the comics department only once. He sat in the far corner of the room from me, sometimes with his hat on, and occasionally glanced at me, pleasantly. On my first day the other faces had not yet come into focus for me. I was busy trying to look competent and accustomed to a high and airy office as part of a big corporation, trying to conceal the fact that I had come from the small office of a small company on a side street. I was just beginning to feel busy and hungry, as lunchtime approached, I was just really beginning to realize the absence of billiards, when Hap, the head with the hat on it, shuffled beefily down the room to my desk. He was a solid, quiet-spoken man who utilized his quietness.

"Coming to the party?" he inquired sweetly.

"Is there a party?" I said.

He nodded. "Luncheon of goodies and things in the board room upstairs and the whole entire complete afternoon off. The works."

"For me?" I said. "A welcome?"

He laughed, in soft separate bursts, and turned to the woman whose desk faced mine. She laughed, too, beating her desk top a couple of times.

"Pretty good," said Hap, his moon-face beaming, and turned back to me. "Don't mean to offend you, but the party's for something else. This is the last working day before Christmas."

The board room was in Spanish style. Out of the ordinary office hallway I entered a small lobby that had black wrought-iron gates. They opened on a huge stucco-walled room with a big hacienda fireplace, which had andirons and pokers and bellows — everything but a chimney. The room was jammed and noisy, and the noise all the more impressive because it bounced off the two-story-high beamed ceiling. A big table down the side was loaded with food. Two small bars at the ends were busy.

This was the moment when I first felt fully the success I had been told was mine. This was my first office party, the first time I had worked for a company substantial enough to have such quarters and to put on such a spread. I felt a glowing bureaucratic snugness at settling into such a big upholstered mechanism, a snugness heightened by the fact that I had an escape hatch — my private work. It was like deep-sea diving with an aqualung. I was down there with the fish, but they were fish and I, swimming about with them, was a human being.

Tappan was run by the three Tappan brothers, sons of long-dead General Tappan who had founded the family fortune with an outhouse monthly called *General Jack's Jamboree.* The Tappan brothers, whom I saw now for the first and last time, were all cast in the same hearty endomorphic mold. They had reputations as hard business men who relied on their seeming stupidity to mask their trading acumen.

During the year they were inaccessible to the staff; not today. I met them soon after I got to the party when they were merely damp-palmed. Later in the afternoon they were sweating, wet, open-collared, hilarious. They dropped ice cubes down women's fronts and backs. They ripped open the buttons on men's flies — zippers were not yet universal — and shouted the scores. (One button was a single, two buttons were a double, three a triple, and four a home run.) Everyone loved it, apparently. I loved it, too, because I was *there.*

About five o'clock I went down to my office to get my overcoat and go home. The room was empty, darkening. Outside Broadway was brightening. It was quiet — New York quiet, which means that the noise was a couple of concentric circles away for the moment. Outside was the city, and around all of us was the Second War. In here, in this high dimming room, I was safe, and within that safety, within my private work, I was even safer.

2

The woman whose desk faced mine was named Peg Molloy. She was in her early thirties, voluptuously built, pigeon-toed, red-headed, small-eyed, generous sometimes, and quick-tempered. She wasn't Irish. Molloy had been a husband along the way, the last of several. She came from an Anglo-Saxon family, very proud of it, that had been ranching in Wyoming ever since the territory was opened. She kept in her drawer, and showed me often, a snapshot of her father and herself when a child, standing in front of horses, with so much space behind them that it seemed as if the picture had no back. That snapshot, in that Broadway building, made her exotic to me. Once she told me that she had come east to go to college. When I asked where, she said, "Chicago." She was the first Westerner I had known. I had met people from California, but that was quite different.

On her desk she often kept a glass of what looked like water, which she sipped from time to time. When it was empty, she stepped out of the office to refill it. I thought she had some sort of dehydrated condition. Then, in my second week or so, I was on her side of the double desk talking to her about something when she took a sip and I got a whiff. Pure gin.

Today that memory seems like half of a Victorian temperance poster, the Before of Before and After. The very last time I saw Peg, some twenty years after I left Tappan, was in a Greenwich Village shop into which she stumbled at nine-thirty in the morning, blind drunk in the maneuverable way that only drinking drunks can manage. I spoke to her and she looked at me. Her eyes took about five seconds to fix on my face, and her mind took another five seconds to remember my name. Her face struggled through puffy anesthesia into pleasure, then she croaked a question about some work I had been doing fifteen years before and had long forgotten. How was it going? I said it was going well and sent my best to her current husband. A few months later I heard that she had died.

But back in the Tappan office she was energetic, scheming, volatile, and giggly. She seemed hard-working but actually she was a sloppy editor with the quick highhandedness of the insecure, and she depended on others, including me, to get her out of jams. She spent a lot of time talking to me about her friends in the literary world ("Bunny" Wilson — I saw a very friendly letter from him) whom she usually met at poker parties, and she also confided in me about her men. She had a lot of quick expeditions, including a judge, but the man she was seeing most was a young intellectual, a sociologist who was insane about her, so much so that he was hostile to me when we met simply because I sat facing Peg all day. But the man she liked more, who eventually became her next husband, was another intellectual, a classical scholar who was in the army overseas in North Africa. I asked her once what she talked about with these types. She said, "Not that goddam intellectual crap" and rumpled her big breasts and giggled. Since she wasn't dumb, her playing the tootsie had its charm.

She showed me the letters of Daniel, the overseas lover, which were exquisitely written and full of very intimate remembrance; she was proud of both aspects. She showed me nude photographs of herself that had been taken by a friend of Dan's, at his request, to send to him. She asked my advice about how she was going to handle Tom, her jealous lover, when Dan came back on leave and for good; and out of my store of worldly wisdom I advised her to make clear to Tom that he was, at most, her man for the duration of the war.

She shrugged and looked dubious. After the next weekend she rushed in — she always rushed — opened her bag and took out three sheets of paper. "You son of a bitch, you gave me an idea for a novel! *Duration Man.* I worked out the whole goddam outline over the weekend." I knew this meant that someone had worked it out with or for her, but I said it was great. I asked when she was going to start writing. "Me?" she said. "Hell, I couldn't write a book. I've made a deal with Sally Frisbee — she's an absolutely top confession writer. I pay her something every week she's working on it and half the take. Hot damn!" She slapped the desk. "I can see the jacket now. *Duration Man* by Peg Molloy!"

The deal was made, but I don't think the book was ever finished. I never heard that it was published.

Peg liked and confided in me for three reasons. She knew I was interested in another girl, so she could talk to me without flirting. She could see that her stories widened my eyes a bit, which she enjoyed. And I helped her with her work when she was late or lazy or fuzzy with hang-over.

And, too, she liked me because she thought I was smart. She admired the fact that I worked an aggregate of about five days in the month. It was about the same amount that she worked, but I accomplished more; and could easily help her when needed.

That was the total time, about five days a month, that it took me to run my three magazines. The rest of the time I did some letter-writing, visited other offices pretending to confer, or fiddled; it's hard work pretending to be busy. But mostly I read. I kept a book in the middle drawer of my desk and read with the drawer open. If a stranger — meaning someone outside our group — came in, I simply slid the drawer shut without touching the book. I read dozens of books that way during my stay at Tappan, while the circulation of my magazines went up and I got con-gratulatory memos and salary raises.

Hap knew I read books, of course. He didn't care a hang as long as the magazines got out on time and sold.

In fact he enjoyed it. His favorite trick was to stop in the hall just outside our door and say, "Oh, Horace, can you come in a moment?" Horace was the editorial director of the whole firm. I would slam my center drawer shut, and Hap would enter alone, grinning at me.

It always worked because once in a while Horace did come in with him, so I played it safe.

Scattered through the months were those forty hours or so in which I talked with my regular freelance scriptwriters and artists and sometimes interviewed new ones; read outlines, made suggestions or disapproved; read scripts and did the same; assigned scripts to artists, checked their sketches and finished pages; and, where the artist's studio hadn't done the lettering of the balloons, assigned the pages to a letterer and proofread the results. Not forgetting the exclamation points. ("Take that, Nazi rats!" "Goot heffens!! Bullets bounce off him!!!") It was all easy. I just thought of the form as frozen film — stills from films. Sometimes I even got an artist to try a montage effect.

But as easy as I found the work, it wasn't my gifts that made *Major Mighty* grow from 600,000 a month, where it was when I took over, to more than 1,000,000 a month in less than a year, that made *Nick Noonday* a contender for the front rank shared by *Major Mighty* with a couple of competitors. Magazines of every kind sold well during the war, and comic books sold phenomenally. Besides the children and others whom they pleased and who now had plenty of pocket money, comic books were the favorite reading of the armed forces. There was a Major Mighty Club, with membership cards and secret code; there were hundreds of thousands of members, about half of whom were servicemen. I saw many a letter from a serviceman overseas confiding his troubles to the Major because there was no one around he could really talk to. I had to answer these "specials." I saw more than one letter from a serviceman overseas applying for membership and asking Major Mighty to rush the membership card so that the soldier or sailor could have it before he went into combat. I didn't write to those men; I had nothing to say. I just airmailed the card myself instead of processing the application through the department that handled routine club stuff.

I took the work seriously during the actual hours, minutes, seconds that I was doing it: my ego was involved. But I didn't see — even remotely — that I was in the middle of something portentous. The war was the immediate cause of the skyrocketing sales, but I was in the middle of an immense cultural shift — the gradual canonization of pop art—and I had no clue. I was in a moderately significant job right in the middle, I was contributing to the shift, and I had no clue.

Nothing that has happened in the elevation of pop art has changed my mind about those comic books, but I certainly was blind about their eventual consequence to others. If it's any comfort to me, so was nearly everyone else. I, in my way, was like all those workers in the Hollywood mills who were just trying to turn out good products and were told twenty years later that, whether they had known it or not then, whether they believed it or not now, they had been creating classics.

Comic books are now regarded with esthetic seriousness by some, not just as sociological data. Particular writers and artists are objects of veneration by collectors, young and old. Recently I went to an exhibition held by such collectors in New York and learned that the period when

I was in the field, before 1950, is now called the Golden
Age. When I left Tappan, I threw away all my copies. I
wish — sometimes, anyway, in common humanity I
wish — I could feel a twinge of regret at what I missed,
instead of thinking it was all either humdrum or funny.

3

There was still another reason why Peg liked me. We
both loathed Colin James. Nobody cared much for Colin,
although some (like Hap) pitied him a little. She and I
loathed him.

Colin was English, in his mid twenties, and tall and fair,
with an airy slow-motion manner and a petty schoolboy
face. His accent was British upper middle class, his family
were civil servants. Why he was in the United States during the war, apparently able-bodied and certainly exempt,
he never explained; rather, he went to some pains to be
mysterious about it with a cozy smile. Despite this coziness
he lived in some terror of the US draft, though he never
explained that either—why he should be subject to the
American draft. He was always importantly busy with the
file of folders he kept between bookends on his desk —
none of the rest of us had anything like it. He was basically remote even when he chose to be friendly and was
always at least patronizing. Usually he was arrogant.

I once suggested to Hap that Colin might be some sort
of British secret agent. Hap smiled wearily and said, "If
that's true, it's going to be a long war."

Colin was good at his work, which insured his place,

and sometimes he came close to conscious parody of his own hauteur, which was amusing. But Peg and I loathed him because he was slimy with his superiors or with anyone who could help him, condescending or cruel with those over whom he had some power. Occasionally we were visited by film people — producers and actors — because Tappan published fan magazines, and visitors to that department were taken on a grand tour of the factory. Colin would always give film visitors the cordial British-gent treatment, would try to fasten on to the party, and often got himself invited to lunch or drinks. With the artists and writers who worked for him, he was silkily overbearing. With the messengers and such, he was pure sahib-with-the-gunbearers.

He had in fact been born in India, where his father had been a minor upcountry colonial official who lived like a rajah. I once asked Colin how he liked India. He shook his head sadly. "The wrong color, you know? And so few of them speak decent English." It was the sort of remark that almost made me like him, it was almost as if he were capable of self-caricature.

But besides the reasons I shared with Peg for disliking him, I had a private reason. He adored his job. He edited three or four of the comic books, the ones with a horror emphasis, and he loved them. He would arrive in the morning with notes he had made during the night, he said, waking up from dreams about his magazines. His folders were full of projects and cross-references. He had long telephone conversations with artists and writers that were as complicated and rhetorical as if he were discussing foreign policy. ("But, my dear Alvin, let's look at it from another aspect for a moment, shall we just? Suppose that the dam had burst *before* Baron Fujimiya fired his super ray. That rather alters matters, doesn't it? Give that some thought over the weekend, will you?") I despised Colin's total immersion in his work; it wasn't true of anyone else in the office, even those who were not leading double lives like mine. I was Anglophile enough to feel that he was desecrating a good English education by not taking the work with several grains of salt. And I may also have been a bit ambiguously uneasy that he was *on* to something, as, in terms of subsequent cultural developments, he certainly proved to be.

So he repelled and disturbed me, for modestly complex reasons, of which his whipcracking was by far the worst. One day a black delivery boy brought him a sandwich from the drugstore on the ground floor. Colin made the boy wait while he opened the sandwich, examined the filling, telephoned downstairs and complained to the manager. Then he said to the boy, "Here's the money for the sandwich since it's here. But I certainly don't intend to tip you for bringing me this garbage." He waved the boy out.

This was only the latest of similar actions. Peg and I decided to build on them. We hatched a plot with Virgil Burmeister, who edited a home-mechanics magazine down the hall, a Midwesterner whose dislike of Colin was heightened by xenophobia. The next time Colin phoned down for a sandwich, our plot clicked into place.

Peg was waiting out at the reception desk for the delivery boy, tipped him and explained a bit of the joke, then took the sandwich out of the bag and replaced it with a well-wrapped three-day-old slice of pizza. I was inside and saw the boy come in with the bag and demand payment before he handed it over. Colin complied, with irritation. The boy left and, under my sidelong glance, Colin opened the bag and the package within. He turned red

ALBUMS OF EARLY LIFE

and white, which he did in continuing alternation when he was furious, and immediately reached for the telephone.

He asked for the drugstore, but the switchboard operator had been primed for Colin's call. Immediately she connected him with Virgil. Peg was in there by now, standing next to Virgil as he answered with a bland "Ye-es?" Colin then launched into a blast about the pig swill he had just received. When he paused for breath, Virgil said grimly, as Peg later told me, "Listen, you limey bastard, it took two men twenty minutes to prepare that food for you, and if you don't shut up and eat it, I'm going to come up there personally and shove every crumb of it down your goddam throat!" Then he hung up.

I saw Colin's jaw wag, saw him fight for air. I saw more red and white. Then he whammed the cradle of his phone and asked for the drugstore again.

This time, as per directions, he *got* the drugstore. When the manager answered, Colin, as he thought, resumed the discussion, at the same pitch. I saw him flinch at the reply. I learned later that the manager very nearly did come up and punch his head, but I had to get out of the room before I burst. Peg and I and Virgil collapsed all over each other in his office. And for days thereafter Colin slunk in and out of the side doors of the building, afraid that the drugstore manager was waiting for him in the lobby.

Time was plentiful, there in the comics department, so Peg and I staged more counterattacks on Colin, though he wasn't aware of them as such. One day he ordered an artist to redraw three pages that had been done on speculation in the first place, as a sample. When the man left, Colin winked at Peg and me and said, "I'll never take them anyway, but the discipline will be good for him." Peg and I looked at each other.

A few days later Colin got a draft notice in the mail. It was obviously a mistake and he expostulated on the telephone three or four times that he was a British national, but he had to go to the board anyway on the specified date to clear it up. He was to be out all morning on the big day. I arranged with an actor friend of mine, Lenny G., who generally played hoods, to come in and sit at Colin's desk, sweep his precious files into a drawer, puff a cigar (Colin hated cigars), and wait. I had explained the reasons, and Lenny agreed that it was all in a good cause.

When Colin returned, he found this unshaven thug, tie pulled down, feet up on the desk, chewing on a big green cigar, looking over some sheets of artwork. Colin went his customary red and white and demanded to know the meaning of all this.

"You were drafted, right?" growled Lenny through his cigar.

"I was *not* drafted!" said Colin hotly, while the red and white continued. "And I'll trouble you, whoever you may be, to get up from my desk."

"Whoever I may be," said Lenny calmly, protecting his turf, "I'm the guy who was hired to replace you." And turned back to his job.

"This is insufferable!" exclaimed Colin. "My files!" exclaimed Colin. "What sort of insufferable nonsense *is* this?" exclaimed Colin. He turned to us, and Peg and I tried to look sympathetic as we bit the insides of our cheeks. "Who *is* this boor?" exclaimed Colin.

"Watch yourself, buddy," said Lenny, quietly.

Colin turned to Hap, whose moon-face showed helpless compassion. Colin looked at me. I looked away as if the

117

spectacle of replacement were too painful. Then Colin said sharply, "Very well. I shall go in directly and take this matter up with Horace Knight." The editorial director.

"Oh, no, you don't, buddy." Lenny had been coached; he was prepared for this move. He got up. "If anyone is going to see Horace, buddy, it's me. I'm the one who's being kicked around here." He strode past Colin, shoving him aside. "You just wait here, buddy boy, if you know what's good for you." Lenny hulked out and, as arranged, went straight to the elevators and left. Colin stood rigid by his desk, more white than red. After a while his impatience got the better of his fear, and he hurried down the hall to Horace's office, where of course Horace's secretary wanted to know what in the world he was talking about.

He came back to our office, furious and curious. He looked sideways around the room with his little sandy eyes and said, "I suppose this was all a joke, yes?" He forced a sick smile as he looked at each of us. "A joke, yes?" We shook our heads in bewilderment and said that all we knew was what we had seen.

This was the first time he had suspected anything; I clinched matters by confessing a few weeks later. Colin's dream had come true: he got an offer to go to Hollywood to work for some fleabag studio on horror and fantasy serials. He was to be a writer and story editor. He was ecstatic, in white and red. On his last day at Tappan, we all went out for drinks with him, to wish him moderately well.

In the drinkiness, I made the mistake of thinking that, because he was leaving and leaving happily, I could tell him what had been happening to him and it might amuse him. He flushed his colors again, but forced a little laugh. A week later my apartment was raided by police detectives. The mayor of New York at the time was La Guardia, the best mayor of my lifetime but a maniac on the subject of betting. Someone had written him an anonymous letter reporting that I was booking horse bets out of my apartment. Subsequently a detective showed me the letter; the phraseology was British.

Colin apparently prospered in sleazy films for as long as I could keep track of him. I never saw any of them, but I spotted his name in trade ads from time to time. Then I heard that he had gone into TV action serials and that he carried some extra weight there because he had been at Tappan in the Golden Age. I'm willing to believe it. Hateful as he was, he was the only one in our office who had convictions about the work. While I was pranking about, bored and slumming and (in a sense) incognito, he was loving it all, with prescience. In cool justice, it was right that he prosper out of it; and that, for more reasons than he was completely conscious of, he hate me.

4

Boredom was the key word. The pranking about Colin was motivated by Colin, but I doubt that I would have put as much time and energy into it if I hadn't been so thoroughly bored with my job and my time-filling around the job. Listening to Peg and drinking after hours with Peg and Hap and Virgil, who was Hap's best friend, were pleasant but nonetheless irritating because I wanted to be out of the world that made me listen to her, drink with them. I progressed at the job, which only irritated me more because it was so easy. The circulation of my magazines continued to grow. I devised an ad for Major Mighty selling war bonds and stamps ("Buy War Stamps and Lick the Other Side") that brought a commendation from the Writers' War Board. With Fred B., who was now freelancing while looking for newspaper work, I cooked up a special issue of *Nick Noonday* — the usual four stories in the issue but with one villain, an issue that could be read as four pieces or one four-part story. Congratulations flowed down from above. (The issue is now a collector's item.) Another raise, to follow the two I had already been given. Success, success. I chafed, relieved only by my other life.

Then, in early 1944, thirteen months after I went to Tappan, I finished the novel I was working on. A publisher took it, which was gratifying; a big magazine bought it for serialization, which was liberating. I resigned from Tappan. When I went in to tell Horace Knight, he asked me to think it over. Just great about my book, great for Tappan too, but I had a future here. I put on my most sincere voice and said I knew it and appreciated it, appreciated what he had done and what I might be leaving, but I had to go. Then he did what bosses often do when you try to resign, he offered me more money — much more than the small raises I had been getting. I hid my anger. (If I was worth the money, why hadn't they been paying it all along?) I thanked him, with double-dip sincerity, but said no.

I continued to see Hap and Peg, but when I left Tappan, I left an environment. To be in comic books and go out into another world at the end of the day was one chemical compound; to be in the other world and never look at it from inside comic books was a quite different compound. After a while, Hap and Peg grew less interested in me, as I in them, No quarrels, no dislike. The geographies of our lives simply filtered apart.

But my connection with comics didn't entirely disappear, for a time. A few weeks after I left Tappan I got a call at home from an artist who had worked for me there. He had been commissioned to draw a daily newspaper strip — six a week — based on the enormously popular radio serial "The Greenbaums." It was a laugh-and-cry soap opera about the rise of an immigrant Jewish family in New York, and Sarah Greenbaum, with her "Yoo-hoo, Mrs. Fine," had become a household word. A syndicate wanted to make a comic strip of the characters, with quite different stories so that one could both listen and read every day. Vera Schwartz, the woman who had invented the serial and who wrote it and also played Sarah, was too busy to write the strip. The artist thought I could easily write the scripts for a week's strips in one morning a week, and, now that I was free-lancing, the magazine money for my novel looked less Himalayan. I accepted.

They liked what I did, and I kept on. In fact I could write a week's scripts in one hour a week. The strip was not a hit, it was never widely syndicated, but I don't think it would have been better if I had worked harder on it. The voices were what people wanted, not drawings and reading matter. As a strip "The Greenbaums" ran less than two years, but for its whole life, I was the script's onlie begetter.

Once every three months I had to confer with Mrs. Schwartz. She had the right of approval of the general story line for each quarter of the year. I conferred with her for the first time in March. Our next meeting was in June—on June 6, to be unforgettably precise. I was to go to the radio studio where they broadcast the day's episode

and, as I had done in March, would sit through the rehearsal and broadcast, then go to lunch with Mrs.
Schwartz.

I didn't. I arrived at the studio that morning to find everything in almost mystical disorder. Everyone was *moving*, talking, chattering, showing papers to one another,
but my impressionistic memory is that all this was very
busy and very silent, like a frantic film with the sound
turned off. I don't know why I had not seen a newspaper
that morning or heard a radio bulletin. I had taken a taxi
to the studio and arrived to find this frenzied limbo. June
6, 1944 was D-day. The Allies were invading Europe.

I spent the whole day in that small radio studio, waiting
for Mrs. Schwartz. The network wasn't sure when they
were going to cut away from news broadcasts to regular
programming. There was no such thing as tape in those
days, all broadcasts were live, so the entire cast of "The
Greenbaums" was kept on tap all day, and I waited with
them. (They never did go on the air that day.) The talk-
back from the control booth was hooked up to the broadcast line, so we could hear the continuing news reports.
Still, people kept sending out for the latest editions of all
the newspapers as they appeared, even though the news
in them was behind what had already been broadcast—as
if print certified what they had heard. That little studio
floor was almost ankle-deep in newspapers by the end of
the day.

At one point in the afternoon I was sitting next to an
actor, an endearing little man famous in the Yiddish theater, who played one of the Greenbaum uncles. He finished his newspaper, possibly his seventh, then turned
and grasped my wrist pleadingly. "You don't t'ink," he
said, "you don't t'ink the whole t'ing could possibly be a fi-
asco?"

It was a question from his soul, his theater soul. I didn't use the word "hit," but I gave him my personal assurance that the invasion would succeed.

It's always tempting to make epitomes out of vivid moments, dramatic conjunctions. I know that my life is not epitomized by the fact that I spent D-day in a radio studio waiting for the broadcast of a soap opera because I was involved in a comic strip. But on particularly depressing days, it's bitterly comfortable to think so. On better days, when I can afford irony, I see it as part of my early success.

Album of a Volunteer Orderly

1

I ENTERED the Second War in New York, late in December 1944, without leaving the city. Up to then I had been doing what most others at home did, odds and ends of civil defense work, as well as saving newspapers for collection, saving fat from cooking and taking it in tin cans to the butcher once a week. I had been deferred twice by the draft board because I had undergone a serious operation in the very week that Germany invaded Poland. I felt fine, but the armed forces were impressed by my long scar. So I did my civilian assistings, and entertained a lot of old friends in uniform when they were on leave. I probably overspent, out of guilt. I certainly felt some guilt, even envy, although not enough to force myself into the merchant marine or some service where my scar would not have been so impressive. Then came the Battle of the Bulge, and my beloved friend John V., who had been an actor with me, who had been wounded in France and had recovered, was killed.

I was glad it wasn't his wife who called with the news. I was glad she was unable to speak. I recognized his sister-in-law's voice at once, but there was a bad connection and I couldn't quite hear her. I thought I understood, but I wasn't quite sure. It was terrible, stupid. I had to ask her to repeat it.

Through the tears in her voice, the words came loudly

like any banal message being shouted over a bad connection. "It's John. John's been killed."

I sat motionless for a while after the call. I knew I was chilled, and I knew I wanted to make some gesture of grief. I wanted to see myself do something. Visible to myself. I wanted to do it before I went out to the memorial service on Long Island that week, I wanted to be able to think about it during the prayers.

I lived at the time a few blocks from St. Vincent's Hospital in Greenwich Village. For months, probably several years, I had seen notices that they needed volunteer orderlies to work part-time because of the manpower shortage. But I had never really read the notices. Now, like so many things that we keep out of focus until we need them, I saw and really read such a notice when I went out later that day, and I walked directly over to St. Vincent's to enroll.

As I went in the door, I asked myself harshly whether this wasn't a movie move, with the music swelling up on the soundtrack. Then I thought of John, his face, the absence of his face, now permanent, and I worried less.

A young nun enrolled me, one of the order of the Sisters of Charity who run St. Vincent's. I told her that I could work evenings. I was assigned three nights a week, a locker, and a gray smock with Volunteer Orderly over my heart. I was told I would have to attend four classes of an hour each before I could begin.

The classes started next night. There were four of us in the group, and we crowded into the small office of Miss Shaughnessy, the head nurse of St. Lawrence Medical. This was a large ward right next to St. Lawrence Surgical.

Miss Shaughnessy almost seemed to fill her office by herself. She was in her thirties, stout, corseted, firm, and funny. First, she explained where volunteers were not allowed to work: surgical wards or operating rooms. "And just to set your minds at rest, or whatever needs to be set at rest, you're not going into any women's wards, either." Her cheery tone conveyed that she was past being bored with jokes on the subject from male volunteers.

We were going to learn some simple jobs: how to take pulse, temperature, and respiration, and how to enter them on the charts. Pulse and temperature were relatively easy; respiration, which the patient could control or become self-conscious about, had to be done cleverly. We would learn how to do a pre-op — the pre-operation body-shaving of a patient. There were instructions about bedpans and urinal bottles. There was advice about where to report what, and where the supply room was. There was warning that prayers were broadcast over the PA system at eccelesiastical hours, that we could kneel and join if we were Catholic, and could simply stand around and wait if we were not. There were special injunctions about respect for the dead, with the note that bodies were never moved downstairs to the mortuary except on the hour, when an elevator had to be reserved for them.

All this advice proved useful.

At our second session a few days later I told Miss Shaughnessy that I had been practicing a lot of pulse-taking and temperature and respiration on a girl I knew. Miss Shaughnessy shook her head and said, "God help her when we teach you enemas."

I passed my instruction course, received a letter of welcome from Sister Loretto Bernard, the head of the hospital, and reported for my first night of duty. I felt superbly responsible. There were nuns in black and white, doctors and nurses in white, student nurses in blue, and myself in gray.

I did well with pulse, temperature, and respiration. I

was quite clever about the respiration count, starting a conversation with the patient, pretending that I was looking at something on his chart, while my hand rested on his chest and I counted his breathing. I moved from bed to bed, feeling like part of a great organism of healing. I handled the urinal bottles with aplomb. Then came the first bedpan.

It doesn't seem ridiculous even now to remember how great a crisis that first bedpan was for me. The struggle never diminished much for me the whole time I worked at St. Vincent's. I saw much more serious things — in a hospital, little could be less serious — but for me each bedpan was a real crisis that I had to force myself to deal with.

It had sounded so easy when Miss Shaughnessy instructed us. The very word "bedpan" was a joke. But I have never been through a more trying few minutes — *never* — than the first time I attended to the bedpan needs, complete with tissue, of a total stranger, an immobilized old Italian with pneumonia.

The only way I could manage it, without heaving, was by thinking of Hitler. I thought of Nazis, and the war, and the horrors. I thought that I was there doing this job, not only because they had drained off people to fight them, not only because they had made John V. disappear forever, not only because I wanted to help a little, but because I wanted to suffer.

This mundane, ludicrous service, which I never got used to, made me suffer. My stomach buzzed with countercurrents of revulsion and control, and I was glad of it. I carried that first pan to the lavatory, covered with a cloth, as I carried very many more, penitently. My good golden friend dead, and I was memorializing him with bedpans. How grateful I was to be sickened.

2

Death came early to me in St. Lawrence Medical. Almost every time I reported for work, a few of the patients would be gone, replaced. Often the missing patient would have been discharged. Sometimes, when I asked Miss Shaughnessy about Mr. X., she would say, "He's gone upstairs." She was a very straightforward woman; that was the only circumlocution I ever heard her use. "Died" was evidently too much even for an experienced nurse, on duty.

We had special instructions about the cardiac patients, about moving them gently when necessary, about not lifting their heads too high, about giving them water, if they asked for it, in a glass with a bent tube so that they need not reach up very far. A few of them were so weak, their pulses so thready (as I knew), that small sandbags were placed between their legs to raise their genitals, to relieve that extra little strain of pumping blood down. Sometimes flannel suspensories were put on them. One night when I arrived, Miss Shaughnessy came out of her office with her mouth pursed and her cheeks flushed in a way that meant she was laughing inside. "I just sent Mr. Y. down to the supply room," she told me, naming another volunteer, "to get a flannel suspensory. The supply clerk just called me up and said, 'What the hell's a flannel suppository?' "

I was rather anxious to see a death. I had seen some dead people elsewhere, but I had never seen anyone die. I thought the hospital would give me the chance, and it

129

would unite me more firmly with my reason for being there. I almost missed it when it first happened.

Pat Riley was a small old man, weak and gentle, with a fringe of very white hair and an oxygen tube strapped into his nose. I had done his chart three or four times and had thought he might float away under my fingers. A week or so after I started at the hospital, I had finished my rounds of pulse and so forth, and was doing other odd jobs when I passed his bed. He raised his eyebrows, his head flat on the pillow, and I knew he was calling me.

"Yes, Mr. Riley," I said, leaning over. "What can I do?"

He whispered meekly, "Could I throuble for a drop of wather?"

I nodded. Carefully, as instructed, I put my arm under his head, raised him a trifle, gently, then turned to pick up the glass with the bent tube on his table. When I turned back to him, his eyes were closed. I was just in time to see him tremble softly, then stop trembling. My arm was under him, holding him, and he had died in it. I felt shocked and grateful. My first death. Accomplished. So lightly, almost pleasantly.

I put down the water he had asked for and would never drink, and put his head back on the pillow. I summoned the nun who was in charge that night. She felt his pulse, touched his eyelids, crossed herself, and went for the doctor on duty.

After the doctor had gone and the curtains had been drawn around Mr. Riley's bed, Sister Theresa asked me to take care of him. "Have you ever done this before?" she asked sympathetically. I said no but that I knew what I was supposed to do. "Well," she said, "let me help you this once."

In her reply I saw many dead men ahead.

One of the main points, I had been told, was to try not to upset other patients when taking care of a man "gone upstairs." Luckily it was night, the lights were low, and many of the patients were sleeping. I went for the basin and the cloth and the towels, and as I returned up the aisle, one little ferrety man with tousled iron-gray hair followed me with his eyes. I smiled to assure him that it wasn't for him. He shook his head slightly, as if he felt it was just a matter of time.

Inside with Mr. Riley and Sister Theresa, I pulled back his sheet and took off his gown — the tube was already out of his nose — and bathed him. He had the body of a boy. I felt biblical, washing and drying him.

Then Sister handed me a large cellophane package. It contained a disposable shroud, made of some heavy paper. I can't remember the exact words, but printed on the package was a catchy trade name, deliberately misspelled, something like Klassy Kut Shrouds. Sanitary. Economical. I took out the paper shroud and, with Sister's help, slipped it onto Mr. Riley.

It was about twenty to eleven. Bodies had to be moved on the hour, I knew, in an otherwise empty elevator. I went out and reserved an elevator for eleven.

On the hour I wheeled Mr. Riley down the aisle, under a sheet, the little ferrety man watching closely. Down went the big elevator to the basement, and I wheeled Mr. Riley into the mortuary, a white-tiled room with rows of refrigerator doors in tiers along one side.

The middle-aged attendant was expecting me. I gave him the form that Sister had filled out, and he snapped it onto a clipboard with a sigh as if Mr. Riley's death were one more he might have prevented, as if it were his fault.

He had a refrigerator already selected, and he helped

me lift Mr. Riley onto the tray he had pulled out. In went Mr. Riley. I could feel that it was cold in there. The door shut. It suddenly seemed terrible that it was dark in there. The fact that there was no light, no thought of a light, seemed to confirm at last that Mr. Riley was dead.

I looked at my watch. "Just three-quarters of an hour ago," I said, "he asked me for a drink of water."

The attendant sighed as if we were the last two people left alive.

The odd thing, I saw later, was that, all this while with a dead man, I had never thought of John. With bedpans, I thought of Hitler and John V. I had to think of them. Here it had been just me and Mr. Riley.

Next time I came in, Miss Shaughnessy said she had heard I had done very well with my first dead person. I decided to be clever. I said I had had death, and men. Was it really a strict rule that volunteers couldn't work with women?

"Oh, you want women, do you? Well, there *is* a place you can work with them. Ambulatory cases. I'll fix it for you."

I knew the difference between ambulatory and ambulance. Miss Shaughnessy sent me to the Emergency Room on the ground floor. I can't remember the first patient, but the second one I helped was a woman, a drunken old derelict, wrinkled and skinny, with bloodied stockings on her matchstick legs. She was stretched on an examining table. "Take off those stockings," the doctor said to me over his shoulder as he worked at the next table.

I had to reach under her skirt and find the tops of those stockings up near the shredded underwear, then pull them down those bruised and gray legs. Then I had to take off the shoes and the stockings and see the feet.

I liked women, the idea of women. I wanted to preserve that.

About fifteen minutes later I was on the telephone to Miss Shaughnessy asking to come back even if they all had died up in St. Lawrence Medical. She chuckled. I was relieved to hear her gloat.

3

My other death, the only other one, came several months later. It was much more frightening than Pat Riley's, but it had a revue-sketch ending.

St. Lawrence Medical was a charity ward, though no one ever called it so. Most men in it paid nothing or very little; most of them were what could still be called working class. One night when I had just reported and done my first rounds, a new patient was wheeled in from Emergency, surrounded by nurses and doctors, and was put in bed. He was quite conscious and calm, and he spoke to those helping him in a highly cultivated manner. He was an electrical engineer, a nurse told me, who lived in a furnished room, had got an infection in his left leg, and for some reason had done nothing about it. His landlady had at last called an ambulance. The intern had taken one look at the leg and had summoned his chief.

I saw the leg now as the chief and a surgeon examined it. It was the color of roast pork and had the same sort of skin. The doctors, I gathered, had no question about whether to amputate. The only question was whether to do it at once or to wait until morning. They decided to let the man, who was middle-aged, rest under medication overnight. He listened attentively as they explained their decision to him.

They instructed the intern on duty to give him an injection, then they left. The intern injected the man, then asked me to get the requisite information from the patient for his chart. Then he left.

I sat on the edge of the bed, with chart and pen, and began asking the man the usual questions. He answered pleasantly. I wondered how a man of his patent intelligence had let an infection develop into gangrene, had lain there watching his leg rot; but I didn't ask that. Just as I wrote one answer and started another question, he suddenly sucked in his breath and lunged upward. I looped my arm around him and grabbed the far side of the mattress, and he kept lunging against my arm, rapidly, like a bucking horse. I thought: Is this what it's like on a battlefield? Is this what one soldier sometimes has to do for another?

Then he gave one last terrific lunge forward. I held him by holding the edge of the bed. Then he fell back. Inert.

All this had taken only about twenty seconds. By the time he had fallen back, the nun in charge had come running from the other end of the long ward. She looked at his staring eyes and felt his pulse and spoke to the student nurse at her side, who went running. The sister knew, and I knew, the man was dead.

Well, I thought, two. Right in my arms. Just like war.

The intern came and confirmed it. He was pale. In a few minutes the medical chief arrived, looked briefly at the man, then called the intern to one side. I couldn't hear them, but they clearly mimed this conversation:

The chief asked, "What did you give him?"

The pale intern replied, "Five ccs. of Such-and-such."

The chief, enraged, said, "I *told* you to give him Thingamabob."

I almost laughed aloud.

I laugh now when I remember it. I still wonder who the dead man was, why he had watched his leg sizzle. I wonder where the intern is. Probably a good doctor somewhere. With no memory of the mystery that he ended, lunging against me.

4

Quiet in the ward. It was late. The last bell for prayers had rung, and the nuns had kneeled among the beds to pray, their flat Bronx and Brooklyn accents murmuring out ancient words from under medieval coifs. They had gone. I was alone with the dim lights, a couple of dozen sleeping men, and two student nurses.

One of the patients was bound with straps on his wrists and ankles to restrainers, those criblike sides that can be attached to hospital beds. He was a dark hairy Czech with a fierce face who had been brought in earlier that day, they told me, after some violent behavior. Something was wrong with his brain, either physical or psychological. Several doctors had voted to send him right to Bellevue, to the mental ward. But the chief brain surgeon, a tall bland Southerner, thought he could handle it. He leaned over the Czech confidently, with a little light to examine the man's eye reflexes, and said, "Now, George, you look rye cheer at this little light." George looked at the light and spit right in the doctor's face. Up shot the doctor, flushed, pointed at the door, and said to the nurse, "Bellevue in the morning!"

Quiet now. Soft dreamy long room. The two blue-clad student nurses were looking over beds and patients at the far end of a restful dim nineteenth-century French painting. I sat down, to riffle a magazine for a few minutes, before my next round of chores. I must have dozed, but surely not as much as a minute.

A cry stabbed me. Even in my doze I knew it was a double cry, fear and suppression of that fear.

At the far end of the aisle stood George, barefoot in his hospital gown, holding a pair of scissors. The two student nurses faced him, huddling together like classic frightened children, staring and round-mouthed.

I got up and started down the aisle.

I suppose there are two kinds of heroes: those who care for some principle more than they care for their lives and those who are the victims of fantasies. I moved down that aisle a hero, but I moved out of all the fiction I had read and all the plays and films I had seen, and I had an added fantasy of gratitude. I had never dreamed, the day I had enrolled there, that I would get a chance at this high pitch.

I could see that the scissors were blunt-ended, the kind that the nurses often carried tucked in the backs of their uniforms. I supposed that George had secretly wriggled free and that when one of the students had leaned over to see how he was, he had reached behind her and grabbed the scissors from her waist.

He saw me coming. The scissors were blunt, but they were scissors.

I started to talk. In the years since then I have often

tried to remember what I said, but I can't recall a sentence, an idea. All I know is that I talked to him continuously, confidentially, and that I kept using his name over and over again. I remember, with a shiver, that I wasn't even remotely afraid. I have never been so brave, before or since. I talked — talked with those two girls watching me, which helped, with many of the patients watching frightened, which helped in another way, with some vague romantic presence in my mind of John, and with finally no control over what I was doing, as if I were aboard a hurtling car that, willy-nilly, rushed me along.

I talked my way up to him and took the hand with the scissors in it as if he had been offering it to me and took the scissors. I didn't even notice it particularly. I was *marvelous*. I saw the girls gasp a little, and, still talking, I put my arm around George's shoulders and talked him back into bed.

When he was once again strapped in, I walked back down the aisle to the cubicle office, as if it were all in a night's work. In a few minutes, after some reassuring of the other patients, one of the students came in, a pretty dimpled girl, blushing. She said something thankful and complimentary.

I brushed it off matter-of-factly, but by that time I could have cried. I felt like a fool. I felt stupid and depressed. What had I to do with bravura actions like that? I felt further away than ever from reality, further and further into dreams that sometimes manifested themselves in ways that pleased others, sometimes not.

5

V-E Day, V-J Day, and everyone's war was over, including mine. As soon as was convenient, I reclaimed my two or three evenings a week. I turned in my smock, and in time I got, unexpectedly, a certificate attesting to my service and a letter of thanks in Christ from Sister Loretto Bernard.

I began to fix the episode in the past of me, as one fixes and mounts a photograph, unforgotten but finished. Then there was a last reprise. One night I was dressing to go to the opera, which one still did immediately after the war if the seats were good enough, when I got a telephone call from Miss Shaughnessy. She said there was a terrible jam, the regular orderlies were sick, the nurses were rushed, and there were five patients in the ward to get pre-ops for the following morning early.

I explained that I was already in a dinner jacket. It was almost quarter to seven and I was to be at the opera house before eight. "Oh, well," she said, "sure. I've got no right at the last minute."

But she hesitated, she didn't rush on to say she would call someone else. And I realized I had debts to her that she didn't know about. "Well," I said, "if you think I can do it in an hour."

I made a phone call of my own, then hurried to the hospital, took off my jacket and shirt, and put on a gray smock. Up in St. Lawrence Medical, Miss Shaughnessy was tending a man whose bed was raised in the front on two blocks. She saw my silk-striped trousers and dress pumps and smiled as we shook hands. "Ah, you're a dear man," she said. "God love you."

"Is that one of the pre-ops?" I asked, indicating the raised bed.

"Who, him?" she said easily. "No, he's just come in to die." The first time I had heard that word from her. She led me down the aisle. "A bleeding ulcer, and he wouldn't stay on his diet. He's been in twice before, and now there's nothing we can do but make him comfortable." I felt funny in my shiny shoes. "No, it's these men down here."

I went right to work shaving their bellies and their pubic hair. I was quite experienced by now. I lathered up each man expertly and worked in sure strokes. Never a cut, never a pull.

It wasn't much more than two months since I had left regular work there, but the whole place seemed very remote. I was there, doing the job well, so I must have known what I was doing, but I could hardly connect with it. The connection, I supposed, the disappeared connection, was the war.

One of the men had a two-inch incision in his abdomen where the surgeon had gone in to do something a few weeks before and would finish it up tomorrow. The wound bubbled slightly as the man breathed and as I shaved around it. I worked serenely, like a retired specialist who had been called back because he was the only one competent for a case.

The last one — the last patient I ever had — was a man who had been operated on some months before for a rupture in his scrotum. To prevent strain, the surgeon had grafted the scrotum to the inside of one leg. Now that the man was healed, the graft was to be cut free.

139

There was just room to get in under the little natural bridge of skin with lather and razor. It was the most difficult pre-op I had ever done, and I did it perfectly. I knew it would be the last of these inappropriate things — inappropriate for my life — that I would do, and I was glad it was the most difficult.

Goodbye, I thought. Goodbye, all you back ends and front ends and pulses and dyings. Goodbye, with thanks.

I never got a chance to say goodbye to Miss Shaughnessy. She was out of the ward on some errand when I finished; and I was late for the opera. I left a word with the sister in charge.

The opera that night was *Rigoletto*. I never enjoyed it more. I never hear it now, not a single strain of it, without a flash of the ward's dim light and the blue student uniforms and Miss Shaughnessy's pink cheeks. Sometimes, too, I hear the voice of John's sister-in-law as I asked her to repeat the message.

Album of a Play Doctor

1

I<small>N</small> 1945 I <small>THOUGHT</small> I <small>WAS A NOVELIST</small>. For ten years, until 1941, I had thought I was a theater man, a member of a repertory company for life, working as one contributor to the production of great plays. That had collapsed. Then for a couple of years I had worked at various magazine jobs to support myself while I wrote novels. Luck with my second novel had allowed me to quit magazine work and to concentrate on writing — novels, mostly. I was hoping to make a long circle back to the theater in some way. Then I suddenly cut across that circle on a short axis.

Claude Leland, who had been in that ten-year theater company with me and had subsequently become a dialogue director in Hollywood, came back to New York to work on a Broadway production. He was assisting Michael Brimmer, a film director in his thirties who wanted to have a hit on Broadway. In those days many Hollywood figures wanted Broadway hits as much for their egos as for their careers, to prove that they weren't mere film people. Michael had signed to direct a play and had brought Claude, who had worked with him on a film. Apparently Michael's theory was that, since he had never directed in the theater, he ought to be prepared for a few tiny problems in which he had no experience: Claude could brief him on them.

Claude called me when he got to New York, and I saw him several times. I was invited to an early rehearsal of the play and met Michael. Then the play opened a pre-Broadway tour in New Haven, and, after four days, it moved to Boston for a couple of scheduled weeks. The night it opened in New Haven it was in trouble. The day after the Boston opening Claude telephoned me and asked whether I could possibly help in the rewriting. I had never done anything like that, but Claude knew me, knew my work, and had recommended me. They had asked him to telephone. I never learned how many they had called before they got to me, but I didn't care. The idea of the enterprise, more than the specifics — being called in to rescue a play on the road, to join in the romance of high-powered show business — was too glittery to resist. I had seen the play, called *Heritage of Glory*, and knew it was no better than its title. Still it would have to have been a lot worse than it was before I would have let it shut me out of this adventure. I told Claude I would come up to Boston and see.

In fact this was not my first brush with big-time show business. While I had been working on magazines, in an office in a tall Broadway building, another friend of mine who had also been a member of that ten-year company was rehearsing in a revue just around the corner. He used to drop in from time to time during rehearsal breaks, and one day he told me that his show needed sketches. I wrote one that night. The director read it the next day and put it in rehearsal. I wrote another sketch that night. The director put it in rehearsal. The day of the dress rehearsal I asked for a contract. The director decided that the show was running long and cut my sketches. The morning after the opening most of the reviews said that the show needed more sketches. But I didn't regret the experience, I was glad of it for a secret reason. Everything about the revue had been the opposite of what I had devoted myself to for ten years, everything about it had given me some of the tingling sensation of sin.

Now again there was excitement, somewhat wicked — even desperate — because this was not the theater I had wanted to work in but, in a perverse way, all the more tingling because of that.

Claude was waiting for me at the Ritz Hotel in Boston. He was a tall, big-nosed, addictedly enthusiastic man with a gassy voice, warm in a puppy-like way and about as reliable as a puppy. He told me as we walked across the Common to the theater that the show was not really in such terrible shape but that the script needed a fresh eye. He and Michael had read my latest novel in California and thought that I was just the man. I couldn't see a connection between my book and this play, but I was careful not to say so. The play had ten more days in Boston before it opened in New York. I would have plenty of time to get the script in shape, said Claude, and it might turn out to be just the break I needed. He knew I wanted to get back into the theater.

In the lobby we met Michael, who embraced me. He was a big, heavyset man with an undershot jaw, full of vigor and quick decisions and bad judgment. (But the bad judgments were all theatrical: he became a successful producer of cheap films.) He wore a flapping seedy topcoat indoors and out, coughed frequently, and carried in one of his topcoat pockets a bottle of cough medicine from which he frequently swigged.

"Great," said Michael as he released me. "Fabulous. I know you can do it, fella. I have great respect for your integrity —" — I had already learned that "integrity" was the show-business term for someone who wouldn't do absolutely anything for money — " — and I know you can really get to the guts of this thing, to the truth. We're going to knit it up and sock it in, fella."

It was curtain time. I went in and saw the play again. It was about the thirty-year-old son of a famous general. The general, who was meant to suggest MacArthur, had died on Bataan; the son, after competent but undistinguished war service, was back in civilian life trying to cope with the public's memory of his father and with his wife's and little son's hero-worship of the old man. The leading role was played by Paddy Quinn, who had been a familiar face in pictures, never a star, during the 1930s and who had been in the theater before and after. He was a bit old for the part, but he was still good-looking and very appealing.

I watched the show and made mental notes. The script was worse than I had remembered. This made me feel fine. I saw, as the thing progressed, how I would slash, rewrite, insert. The work would have been harder for a better play. The show went by like a patient on a stretcher, and I was the surgeon who would operate. The worse the case, the more I would shine.

Later that night there was a meeting in Bernie Manheim's suite at the Ritz. Bernie was the producer. He was also a sailor in the US Navy. It was now only a few months after the war's end, and Bernie had not yet been discharged. He had enlisted in the navy three years before because he had connections and could get himself stationed at Church Street in New York with light duty.

Bernie looked like a thug. He had a bull chest, a flat nose, a truculent mouth, and he walked with his hands usually clenched in fists. His voice and his speech were like an assault. The paradox of his face was his gray eyes, which were beautiful. I had heard stories from Claude and others, often told with a proud grin, that Bernie had been a top mobster in the wholesale produce markets and was very rich, that he had been in various troubles with the police and once had narrowly escaped a murder charge. True or not, the stories didn't strain belief.

Bernie had arrived at the Ritz while I was at the performance. His pea jacket and sailor hat were on the sofa next to him. He and I had met before, and he shook hands with scowling seriousness. Zack Someroff, the business manager of the production was with him. Zack was a sweet-faced dimpled man, witty, formerly handsome, now fat with compulsive eating. Bernie ordered sandwiches, to go with the drinks already in the room, and Zack ate most of the food, chuckling and shrugging as he attacked each fresh sandwich.

We talked generally for a little while with Claude hovering on the outside of the circle supplying an "ooh" or an "aah" whenever I said anything. Bernie was impressed with me, not because he had read either of my novels but because he had seen my name on the jackets. Zack was on my side because he liked me — we, too, had met before — and because I reminded him of a cousin of his who was a successful playwright-director. Anyway Zack was willing to try anything, more out of indifference than pressure. He didn't give much of a damn about the show, despite the fact that he did his job excellently. He was getting paid very well, and he knew the whole thing was a tax write-off for Bernie.

Very soon Bernie said, "OK, let's cut the ———— already." He said to me, "The thing, the whole thing is, do you think you can improve this ——————— show?"

I said, "Bernie, a child of five could improve it. I can

145

improve it about two hundred per cent, I guess, at a minimum, but I'm not sure that then it will really be any good."

Zack chuckled in his disarming way, as if this scene, like all of his life, were being performed for his amusement. "If you made it too good," he said, "you'd only upset Bernie's accountants. Just make it good enough to bring in." To New York, of course. "So we don't look like total slobs. What you saw tonight we just can't bring in."

"How much time do we have?" I asked.

Michael decided it was time to make his presence felt. "Not much. But I've been working out a rehearsal schedule —"

"Wait a minute," said Bernie, "what's not much?" To me he said, "I already discussed with Zack. We'll close Saturday here. We'll save here a week. Tomorrow Zack calls Marvin." Marvin was the manager of the Broadway house they had booked. "We'll see whether we can put off for a week the opening, at half rent. That ———————— owes me a favor. I got him that red-headed usher he's banging these days, right this moment, I bet. He owes me one."

Zack smiled benignly at me. "Now you're in show business."

"Not quite yet," I said. "That would give me a week to do the revision. Then you'd have only a week to rehearse it."

Michael said, "You can feed me the new stuff next week while you're doing it. I can work with the cast while you're finishing."

Zack said, "I'll get you a room in Mike's hotel in New York. You live at home, if you want, but you work in the room down the hall from Mike."

It was moving fast, it was whirling around me, I was the

center. I loved it. I felt I had been born for the moment.

"What about the author?" I asked. "Does he agree about my stepping in like this?"

Bernie snarled between his teeth. "That stupid ----------. I sent that stupid ---- back to New York. Tomorrow I send him home to Chicago. He opens his ------- mouth, I'll tear off his ----- and shove it down his ------- throat."

Zack looked at me sweetly. "OK?"

I laughed. "I'd still like to have something on paper, something the author signs."

Michael agreed gravely. "He should have it, Bernie. He should be protected."

Impatiently, Bernie said, "Zack, you'll get?"

"I'll draw up something in the morning and send it to his agent. It'll be easy. He doesn't sign, we close for good. Our way, he saves something."

Bernie turned to me like a bulldog ready to bite. "Well?"

"All right," I said, announcing a decision I had made the moment Claude telephoned me in New York. "I'll do it."

Michael coughed happily and swigged at the medicine he took from his topcoat pocket. "Fabulous," he wheezed. Behind him Claude glowed.

Zack, who had known all along, I thought, that I would agree, said, "Bernie, Stanley's going to need a little money to go on, pocket money."

Obviously, when someone asked Bernie for money, his first instinct was to fight. But he quickly saw the justice of this request, and the scowl cleared. "OK. So how much?"

"A hundred," said Zack.

"What?" snarled Bernie.

"You heard me," said Zack, "fifty dollars." He glanced at me and smiled as if to say, "I tried."

Bernie grunted and pulled up his navy blouse. Tucked into the waistband of his tight trousers were his wallet and his checkbook. "I'll give a check."

The sailor with the thick neck bent over the endtable next to his chair and, under the lamplight, scribbled me into the Broadway theater.

2

I floated. For the next few days in Boston, for the next two weeks in New York, I was lofted beyond the tugs of circumstance. I felt that I had sailed into my sphere, that my predestined life had been realized.

The members of the cast welcomed me with hardly a grumble. Partly this was because they knew they were in trouble and help of some kind was needed. Partly it was because Claude had propagandized for me, partly because Zack told them I reminded him of his famous cousin when young, partly because Michael had a rapidly swelling sense of incompetence and wanted to get out from under a looming disaster by building me up as competent, therefore responsible. And partly it was because from the very beginning I did things to the script that showed a grip.

The only one who disliked me was an ancient actress named Florence Forbes — I had books at home with pictures of her as an ingenue in the 1890s — who played the hero's mother, widow of the great general. I disliked her first. She looked like the hero's grandmother, and she played the role with every cliché she could remember and many that she didn't have to think of because they were second nature to her. She was an old theater animal and must have scented my dislike of her under my restraint. Her dislike worked itself out by affecting her memory for new lines which, before my coming, she had handled well. The last night in Boston she took her little grandson on her lap, intending to console him with my new line, "Things look gloomy now, darling, but don't worry, it's all passing." What she said was, "Things look gloomy now, darling, but don't worry, it's all permanent."

And the two lady furniture-movers were aloof. They had a brief scene that had been written in to get a few laughs out of the wartime manpower shortage. The scene wasn't funny and would have stuck out as padding even if it were funny. One of the first things I told Michael and Zack was that I was going to cut the scene. I told them confidentially, but the two actresses caught the whiff in the air and looked at me like a hired assassin.

Otherwise it was creamy. Paddy, a lean-faced Irish-American, full of twinkling-eyed deployable charm, took to me at once; and I, who had watched him from movie balconies in my high-school days, was entranced. Even the boy who played his son, Dennis Feeney, a freckle-faced kid who was a freckle-faced kid in lots of magazine ads, liked me somewhat — the first time that a child had responded reasonably well to me. I thought it was because I was just getting old enough — close to thirty — to be interested in a child as a child. The feeling had doubtless been delayed in me because I had no children of my own.

By the time we were all on the train coming down from Boston, we were full of the elation of triumphant return

149

although we all knew that we were facing a week's pause while I finished rewriting the script. Marvin, the Broadway theater manager, had agreed to a week's postponement of the opening so that they would have some time to rehearse the new script. That railroad car was suffused with the Spirit of the Second Chance.

Somewhere south of Providence, while Paddy was doubling me up with foxy inside stories about Hollywood figures he had known, Zack came down the aisle and waved his hand at me, a hand just as plump and dimpled as his face. "Can I wangle you away from that drunken Irish con man for a minute?" Paddy, holding bottle and paper cup, said with cartoon booziness, "Watch out who you're calling Irish." I laughed, convinced that at last I knew the meaning of the phrase "best of all possible worlds," and went with Zack.

In a compartment were Bernie and Michael and some glasses. We all had drinks and came quickly to the point. They didn't want me to make any plans for the week after the week in which I finished rewriting the play. They wanted me to be around to comment and observe and polish when they went back into rehearsal, and they would pay me for my time. I asked Michael whether he would mind, and he said, "Hell, fella, I'm the one who suggested it." Bankruptcy, I thought, as generosity. "You've got ideas," said Michael. "We want you to stick around and keep on being creative. Besides, you get a production credit, and you can use that, right?"

I said I was grateful, but within myself I was only patient. This was my realm; they were all courtiers.

What I remember most clearly about the week of rewriting are the praise and the club sandwiches. I can't remember the actual writing. The pages spun through the machine — better, certainly, than they had been. I had lunch in the room every day, a club sandwich. I handed clumps of sheets every day to Michael and Zack — Sailor Bernie kept away — and Michael kept shaking his head in tight-lipped Hollywood awe and Zack just kept dimpling. I went home at night, tired but almost too happy to sleep, anxious to get back to the hotel room next morning and write some more and get some more praise.

I never had an easier week. Some twenty-five people were waiting for me, a Broadway theater was waiting for me, and all I felt was carefree. My ten years in the repertory company had prepared me for all this, in a way, by setting me above it. I would pass through this success, tolerant of those to whom it meant everything, to another side, to more.

I finished the rewriting about noon on Saturday, and the last clump of pages was duplicated that afternoon. Early that evening there was a meeting in Zack's office, up an archaic elevator in a fusty building on a street off Broadway. There was Bernie, sitting behind a desk in his sailor suit, looking like a Goth who had conquered the city. Zack was in a chair near him. Michael and Claude sat on a dying sofa, Michael in his topcoat coughing sagely, Claude glowing, his very clasped hands glowing.

Zack, though not behind the desk, was chairman as usual. He said to me, sweetly quiet, "You honestly did a fabulous job."

"Fabulous, fella," said Michael.

"Just what we expected," said Zack. He smiled and shrugged: "Well, what we know now we expected. Anyway, we think the show stands a chance now — not just not to get murdered but maybe to stick around a couple of months. But we all think it needs a fresh viewpoint.

The production, I mean. And we think you should take over as director. Bernie agrees, Mike agrees."

Bernie nodded sullenly, which merely meant that he didn't really know what he was nodding about and was as usual being guided by Zack. Michael said, "We have confidence in you. And I'm going to be standing by. You can count on me."

Silently I flung an obscene reply at him. "Thank you, Mike," I said.

"Now you're thinking about program credit," said Zack. I wasn't but I would have been, and I was glad he had mentioned it. "By contract Mike is director, but a good prominent production-assistant credit for you."

"Fine."

"And I've got an agreement I'll send on Monday to your agent," said Zack. "Covers the rewriting, the redirecting."

"Fine," I said, knowing that I would have gone ahead, as I had been working, without a contract. "What about the cast? What about Florence? I don't think she cares for me."

Michael said, "We've got a surprise for you. We gave Florence her notice and we sent some of your pages to Rose Mackaye. She likes it. She starts Monday." Rose Mackaye was one of the best elderly actresses in New York, a woman I had loved ever since I had been going to the theater. I said so.

"Then we're off and running," said Zack. He smiled with dimpled caution. "Well, anyway off. The cast gets the rest of the new script tonight, Monday we begin. We've got a week. Alleygazam."

"I think we can do it," I said. "At least they know the characters, they know the set, and so on. If they cooperate, I think we can do it."

"If they don't," said Bernie, "I will personally tear off their ----- and ----- and shove 'em down their ------- throats."

So, at ten o'clock on Monday morning, I went into the Commodore Theater as the director.

3

It smelled good. There were two smells, in fact: the high mustiness backstage, the damp hushed lake smell of the front of the house when empty. I had never felt more at home in my life than the morning I walked in there, less wary of any work I was starting.

The company was mine. They had read the new script, knew it was much better, and had already learned most of it. They had done some reading on the earlier parts during the past week with Michael, but, as Paddy told me, without much reliance on his direction. During that week I had seen a few of them for dinner, like Paddy, and we had got on well. Now they looked at me as if I were the doctor who had fought his way through the blizzard with the serum.

Every minute, every hour increased my confidence and theirs in me. I had directed before, in various places, and now as before, I modeled my behavior as well as my methods on the director of the company I had been in for ten years. I hated him for the dissolution of the company, but I knew how good a director he was in many ways, and I had a species of revenge by using what I had learned from him here in a theater he had despised. So for the first day or so I put a chair for myself on stage in front of the footlights and sat there speaking quietly to the actors as we worked out new patterns of movement, new integrations of relationships, taking an actor aside if there were major points to be made so as not to embarrass him. I knew I was a better director than my model, more evocative, less imposing. I could see it working on the actors.

Claude, when he wasn't running errands or helping otherwise, sat in the front row of the orchestra, wide-eyed, yessing me even when he was silent. Zack dimpled at me and in the lunch-breaks tried almost frantically to be funny but was hampered by his respect. Michael dropped in from time to time during the week, sitting in the back of the house, nodding approvingly when I passed as if, by remote control, he was operating through me. Bernie blushed when we met in the wings, unused to being pleasant and satisfied. Rose Mackaye, the lovely old actress who was now the grandmother, wrote me a note — I got it at home five days after rehearsals started — telling me how much she thought of me. Paddy addressed me in Yiddish terms of endearment, phrases he had picked up in Hollywood.

Only little Dennis Feeney, the grandson, was impervious. Obedient but impervious. Nothing bothered or impressed him. He had the notorious sang-froid of the professional child that drives mature actors mad — no trace of stage fright, instant memory of his lines and of everyone's lines. Dennis was never flustered and was always, unembarrassedly, phony. He was a photographer's model, and he could make any kind of face that he was asked for. This was the first acting he had ever done, and he just kept on making faces.

The only human thing I knew about this little manufacturer of barefoot-boy appeal was that when Zack had taken him and his mother and his agent to lunch at a good restaurant, to settle Dennis's contract, the boy had been invited to order what he liked from the grand menu and he had asked for a cream-cheese-and-jelly sandwich. I clung to that story as a thread of hope in the moments when he was obeying me impenetrably.

While the set was being installed and touched up at the Commodore, while the lights were being hung, we had to rehearse elsewhere. Zack got us a theater down on Second Avenue, in those days a Yiddish theater, which was between shows. The fact that we were going down there for a few days couldn't have suited Paddy better. At the first rehearsal on that stage he came out with his hat on, beating his breast with his fist, nodding his head, and played his first scene with a sour-cream accent, while the rest of us rolled with laughter.

It was an immense theater, used mostly for musicals, and there was a wide orchestra pit full of battered music stands and chairs. One morning we rehearsed Dennis's big emotional scene, in the course of which he went from Face and Voice A to Face and Voice B, and so on, all patently prepared in front of the mirror and his mother. I watched from the middle of the house, wondering how I could crack through that juvenile glacier. I thought of the cream cheese and jelly. After the scene I came down the aisle to the orchestra rail and called him to the footlights. Speaking across the orchestra pit, I explained quietly, while he listened with complete attention, that we didn't want him to "show" us anything, we just wanted him to understand what this other little boy was feeling and the rest would follow, that we knew he could do it because this other little boy was very much like himself and probably liked the same kinds of sandwiches, and so on. He listened unwaveringly. I finished and asked him whether he agreed. "Yes, Mr. Kauffmann," he said soberly, then continued without a break, "Mr. Kauffmann, do you think this pit is about eight feet wide?"

The set was ready at the Commodore; we went back uptown. Euphoria reigned. Everyone knew, which was true, that the show was getting better and better. *"King Lear* it ain't," said Paddy. "Maybe not even *The Cherry Pickers*. But at least now the curtain goes up and down right, and we don't bump into each other." He thought it was better than that. So did the others.

Euphoria then took the form of a small celebration for Bernie. He had given the cast a week's layoff at full salary while I rewrote the play and another week at full salary while we rehearsed. We all knew it was a tax loss for him, but it was a tax loss that had helped us. We all contributed to buy him a gift, which we presented to him after the first dress rehearsal. We gathered on stage, and after a few minutes Zack brought Bernie in, flushed and disconcerted. Later I learned that Bernie wasn't flushed with modesty: Zack had found him busy with the red-headed usher in the ushers' dressing closet.

"Bernie," said Zack, dimpling, as we gathered around the chunky sailor, "at first we thought we'd get you something for your money, but we couldn't find a big enough trunk." Laughter. Bernie ducked his head, trying to behave the way he thought people ought to behave when they were being amiably kidded. Then Zack gave him a nicely wrapped present — some ties for civilian life — and we all applauded and Bernie tried to thank us without using profanity.

As the celebration was breaking up, Michael slipped an envelope into my hand, with a look of friendship on his lantern-jawed vulpine face that would have done little

Dennis proud. When I got off by myself, I opened the envelope and found a three-page handwritten letter on Michael's hotel stationery. It began: "Dear Stan, Three weeks ago I made a friend." It wound on and on through its explicit praise and its implicit self-protection. Michael's name was on the program as director, mine was merely noted with thanks for my assistance. Michael was signaling that, in case the show was a hit or at least got some favorable publicity, he wanted me as partner, not insurrectionist. Yet the letter was so neatly phrased that he had no future obligation to me if things went badly. It was well done.

That first dress rehearsal had gone smoothly. The second dress rehearsal went better. The audience was enthusiastic — not a full preview audience, just a couple of dozen people whom Zack had rounded up somewhere. Every laugh line got a laugh, every curtain brought applause. The air hummed backstage.

Then we opened.

4

Early the next morning I went out for some breakfast groceries. I felt that the few people in the street had read the reviews and were staring at me. Later I went out to get some things for lunch. I felt that the many people in the street were staring at me. When I went up to the theater that evening I thought that the crowds on Broadway were turning their backs on me and were looking at me over their shoulders.

In the theater itself the stagehands were consoling, the

company sore but plucky. Rose Mackaye kissed me and gave me a flower for my buttonhole that she had brought from her window box at home. Michael and Claude didn't come around until the next day. Michael looked like a captain who had given a lieutenant a chance that had been bobbled. "That's the Army, lad," his look seemed to say. "Shape up or ship out." Claude seemed to keep himself behind Michael at all times, looking over Michael's shoulder at me in sorrowful moist-eyed agreement. Bernie had disappeared. He had disappeared about halfway through the party after the opening at the luxe Central Park West apartment of a business friend of his, a partial backer of the show. When the reviews started to come in, Bernie had begun to get sloppily drunk. His wife, a birdy dyed blonde, had dragged the heavy sailor away. I never saw him again.

The reviews had been characteristically incompetent to discern the good elements in the show, like some of the performances, but in sum they were not unjust. They could not have been just to me because they could not take into account the script and the staging with which I had started. How often I and others had told ourselves not to see the improvements disproportionately. How little effect our own warnings had made on us.

Still one review infuriated me. It gave me a point to fume righteously about while everything else disintegrated. I asked Zack whether we should write to the editor of the *Evening Blade.* Their critic had arrived somewhat drunk and had panned the show like all the rest of the press, but he had added that the worst scene was the one with the lady furniture-movers. The scene that had been cut out in Boston. This critic had evidently read the out-of-town reviews, which had singled out that scene for dispraise, and then had dozed through opening night. It was blatant dereliction, I said, and I thought it ought to be charged.

"Forget it," said Zack gently. "He's always drunk. It's a blessing if you've got a hit because he just rewrites other people's raves. The rest of the time you take your chances."

"But should we let him get away with this?"

"We can't win anything," said Zack. "We'll only look like soreheads. Suppose we prove our point. How's it going to help us?" He was pragmatically right; but his "we," I thought, excluded me. He was thinking of his own future shows. He dimpled a smile at me. "Of course we could always get Bernie to go over to his office and tear off his ———— and shove it down his ——————— throat."

The play closed on Saturday night after five performances. Only after it closed did I realize that the author, so far as I knew, had not been at any of those performances. He had gone back to Chicago after Bernie had given him an ultimatum.

The Monday after the closing Michael and Claude went back to California. Michael called me from his hotel just before he left and said he was short of cash. Could I meet him at Grand Central — in those days the chic route was Twentieth Century Limited and Santa Fe Chief — and lend him a hundred and ten dollars? He would mail me a check as soon as he got home. I didn't ask the reason for the odd figure, and he didn't tell me. I felt some kind of bruised loyalty and I happened to have the money, so I got it out of the bank and went up to the station. He and Claude bade me farewell as if we were all campaigners who had been together on St. Crispin's Day and shared a secret that others would never understand.

Zack kept in touch. He said he would try to get me more directing work, possibly through his cousin. I knew that he understood my feeling about myself, and, at least to some degree, shared it, the feeling during rehearsals that I was a king in my kingdom. "A little bit of leverage," said Zack later on, "it's happened for worse shows, and you'd have had a foot in the door." He kept his word and did try for a while to help me, but the world piled up on him, and he didn't have much to go on in my case. He waddled smilingly out of my life. He died about ten years later of, I heard, overeating.

Dennis Feeney went into films, made two, and failed. The era of child stars was ending; besides, the camera magnified his cue-card face-making.

Paddy and I remained friends for about four years, and through him I met a number of film actors — some of them from silent films, some of them ex-stars — who formed a small freemasonry in New York. Being with them was like being belatedly behind the scenes at matters that had been important to me when I was ten and fifteen. But we parted. Paddy and his friends were either politically conservative or politically null, and although I was not a radical, I seemed so to them. They dropped me, almost with a screech, as the heyday of Joe McCarthy dawned.

Bernie produced two successful musicals in the next decade and a few failures. Then he went into other tangential business and, with the aid of a public relations firm, tried to make himself into an avuncular New York figure. I never got a penny from him for all the work I did other than the first fifty dollars in Boston.

Michael went on to his millionaire success as a producer of exploitation films. He never sent back the hundred and ten.

Claude rang me up some years later when he came to New York, but the sound of his voice reminded me of those sad eyes looking over Michael's shoulder and I invented some reason not to see him.

As for me, I was haunted by the idea of poetic justice, as if I had been punished for straying from the kind of theater to which I had once devoted myself. In one way I disliked the idea because it was possibly priggish, but mostly I was proud of it because I had really known such a devotion: and it could now mark me out for such a high idea as poetic justice.

Proud or not, right or not, I was homeless again. I had to find another country in which to be a citizen, let alone a king.

THREE

Album of Suicides

1

I'VE KNOWN THREE WOMEN WHO ATTEMPTED SUICIDE, two of whom were eventually successful. All were beautiful.

Nan Talbot worked in a publishing house, an editor before I became an editor there. She was incompetent. It was a firm of paperbound reprinters, and she had been engaged some months before I arrived to select and handle books for women. Apparently the bosses had thought that her womanliness would compensate for her lack of editorial experience. They may even have thought that her average taste would be useful in the job.

Her appearance was not average. She looked queenly. She was tall and erect and she had the figure of a showgirl. She moved deliberately and smoothly, like a royal barge. She had blonde hair and deep-set eyes and the whitest teeth I have ever seen. Her face was like a magazine illustration tempered by something blunter. Later I learned that she had some Indian blood: I thought it was visible.

I met her on Valentine's Day 1949, the day I started in publishing. She welcomed me like a housemother: she hoped that I would be happy there. I noticed that her eyes sometimes went up to the ceiling while she talked to me, to anyone.

By the time I arrived, one of the top men in the firm had already made a play for her. She told me this later, and told me that after a while she had permitted him, once, to succeed. ("Let him do his business" was her phrase.) She never suspected, as I did, that she had been hired because she was attractive and one or another of the top men had ticked her off as a private possibility. She was so used to attention that she thought it quite natural, quite incidental and inevitable, that men would move toward her. She thought this without vanity.

But facile male attention enraged her. Women in those days still joked and bragged about being whistled at in the streets. It often happened to Nan, and she hated it. She would tell me about it angrily, her jaw clenched, her face flushed and tight.

She confided in me and in one other man in the office because she saw early that neither of us was moving toward her and she could talk more easily to men than to women. Within a few months the other man quit the firm, leaving his wife to go off with another woman who worked in the office, so I was then Nan's only confidant. This confiding took place partly at lunch, which we had together about once a week, but mostly it was in long typewritten letters, which I would hear her whacking out in her office and which she would then hand to me, folded, without envelopes. Two or three of them a week.

I soon thought the letters were boring, but then I thought she was rather boring. Still she was so frank, she assumed so completely that I would respond, that I hadn't the heart to avoid listening and reading. Besides, I was bored by the job, as I had been by most office jobs, and she helped to pass the time. She really didn't want anything from me, least of all advice, she just wanted an ear or an eye. And the boredom of her talk and letters was at least a change from the work that drained my time away so that I could get money to support my own work for a few hours every day before I came to the office.

Love and sex were the two chief themes in Nan's talk and letters. The job and its difficulties were a close third — not her difficulties in doing it but with the slights she imagined all around. I was more interested in the first two subjects. She had been divorced twice. She came from a prim Ohio family and had married in her sophomore year at college, a marine officer. They broke up three months later, but it was enough to finish her college career. Then came some rousting around, various cities, various jobs, various men. Then she married a young businessman with whom she tried to have a child, without success. They had gone to specialists in America and Europe, who had told them there was nothing wrong with either of them. She had had internal adjustments. Still no child. After four years her husband divorced her and produced children with another wife.

Nan felt failed, angry, unrealized. She read a best seller about self-confidence by a popular New York psychoanalyst, then went to him as a patient. Within a month he made love to her on the office couch. She told me about it merely with puzzlement, nothing like the rage with which she reported the whistlings in the street. (For her, sex was always something a man did to a woman. "After he did his business, we just went on talking.") Again she took his actions quite calmly as the effect of her looks, and she kept going to him professionally. She was still going to him. I tried to make her angry at him, but she couldn't get much more than puzzled.

Her troubles at the job arose because she was no good at it and, although she didn't know this, she was sufficiently uneasy to see insults everywhere. She could do just well enough, in her reports and recommendations and the copy she was supposed to write for covers and inside pages, so that others could patch them into usability.

167

I suppose that in time, after the boss who had slept with her was embarrassed enough at having her around and was exasperated enough by her incompetence, she would have been fired. Meanwhile she worked hard and, like all incompetents, kept asking how she was doing. And kept being offended by trifles.

She tried to improve herself, and this led to complications in her private life. When I arrived, she was having an affair with a young engineer named Willis, whom I met, pleasant but with one of those faces it takes a while to remember. She wanted to marry him. He wanted to keep things as they were. She loved him, she told me; and thought he would make a good husband; and, although she let him keep doing it, she didn't like being phoned whenever he felt like spending a night or a weekend with her. This had been going on — before and after the boss's and the psychoanalyst's attentions — for a couple of years. Then Nan decided to take an evening course in writing at N.Y.U. to help her in her work. There she met Gareth, a young writer from Kentucky.

A few weeks later a long letter was handed to me. The young writer had taken her home the previous night after class and had gone to bed with her. "He did his business, and it was the best s-e-x of all my born days (Or do I mean nights????) I still love Willis, but Gareth is simply tuh-riffic!!! What to do? Ah, me."

Gareth called for her at the office one day, and I was introduced. He was taciturn, mustached, with a crew cut and the eyes of a killer snake. (He is now a well-known novelist.) He was icily impressive.

He kept seeing Nan when she wasn't seeing Willis. Willis wasn't closely attentive at best, and she made sure that he didn't come around on the two class nights every week. I was glad of Gareth in a selfish way because it gave some novelty to the letters.

Nan hoped, though she didn't precisely say so, that the fact of Gareth would jog Willis into proposing. Although she made sure the two men didn't meet, she made a great honest point of telling Willis about the other man. It had just the effect she didn't want. Willis said she was free to live her own life, as was he. So she was cheated of her "Ah, me" dilemma. She was left with a man she wanted as a husband and a man she couldn't resist as a lover, both of whom visited when they chose.

She kept her outward calm, though she was more and more distressed. I could see the distress in the letters was genuine though they always sounded as if they had been typed in a chintz-curtained college dormitory room with one leg folded under her. She moved carefully, with the sobriety of a practiced drunk, but her only alcohol was insecurity. She let herself flare into hot red tempers only when she was telling me about insults: otherwise she sailed gracefully and said "Mm-hm" a lot and glanced at the ceiling.

Sometimes, especially when she was angry, I felt remorse for the way I thought of her. But I paid for it with my time. Gladly, because it helped to pass the time.

The writing course ended, and Gareth went home to Kentucky. In an odd way this made the situation worse for Nan. It wasn't because she missed Gareth: Willis "did his business" well enough, even though it wasn't as "tuh-riffic" as with Gareth. What was worse was that now, more intensely than before, she was dependent on Willis. She loved him, she had loved him all along and had never loved Gareth, Willis was the one she could see herself in the same house with all her life, and now she felt even more at the mercy of his whim. "I don't care if he has other girls," she wrote, "I wouldn't even care after we were married. (Shocking???) If we ever are. But he treats me so casual. (Casually?) He's always got a good reason why I haven't heard from him in a week, but the darned fact still remains that I haven't heard from him in a week. Golly." And she appeared in my office doorway, as she usually did about fifteen minutes after she had handed me a letter, to see whether I had yet read it, moving carefully, looking gorgeous and wise and quite unconnected with the letter she was wondering about.

I foresaw endless letters. I had bouts of panic when I thought that the tedium would outweigh the diversion. But there was no way out of it now. I was trapped.

She released me. One Friday afternoon after work, we rode downtown together on the bus. It was accidental: I usually went home another way. I forget what we talked about, but I remember being surprised that it was something other than herself and her troubles. She got off first, saying "See you Monday."

On Monday she wasn't there: she was in the Bellevue emergency ward. She had gone straight home from the bus, taken thirty sleeping pills, turned on WQXR, the classical music station, then had lain on her bed. The first real pang I ever felt about her was not about the pills because, by the time I heard about them, it was she, recovered, who was telling me. The pang was WQXR. She wanted to be found with good music playing on the radio.

She had done it because Willis had promised to call her before three that Friday afternoon at the office, to tell her whether he was coming for the weekend. So her mind had been made up all the while we were chatting on the bus. Willis came around on Saturday afternoon, heard the radio, went away, came back, heard the radio, got the superintendent to let him in, found her and rushed her to Bellevue.

She told me the story a week later. She had circles under her eyes but otherwise looked the same. She told it without any drama, talking about the Bellevue ward as if she had gone to a beauty parlor. I remember thinking, "My God, you can go over the edge for good, as far as you know, and still come back dull."

I think she believed it was for good. I don't think the suicide attempt was a trick: I don't think she was wily enough. Besides, she couldn't have been sure that Willis was coming. But it had the effect of a trick. Willis proposed. That solved one problem. He wanted to move to Massachusetts. That solved two other problems, her incompetence and my entrapment. They married and moved, and in three months she was pregnant. "My poor ole noggin just can't figure it out," she wrote. (Her letters continued for a while, by mail.) "After all that stretching and tube-blowing and all those doctors with Howard" (her second husband). She visited New York about a year after her child was born, and we had lunch. She had a son. Willis was an attentive father and a good husband. Gareth had not even sent a card when the baby was born though she had written to tell him. "I sure made the right choice," she said, though I couldn't see that she had chosen. She missed the job and being busy, "the gang." As soon as the baby was old enough, she was going to try for a job in the town bookshop.

We fell out of touch. By mail she was easier to discourage, simply by delaying replies and finally not replying. Then one day in the late 1960s I got a note from her. She was coming to New York. Could we have a drink? I felt guilty enough, even curious enough, to reply and to agree.

When she came into the bar, she sailed up to me, with the same stately smooth glide. She held out her hand as if she were receiving me. She was heavier but still beautiful. She still glanced at the ceiling from time to time as we talked. Willis was doing well and was still a good husband. She was the assistant manager of the bookshop. Her son was eighteen and very troublesome, running around, taking drugs. Nan hated him. She flushed when she said it, her jaw clenched.

2

Betty Berger came to work as a secretary about a year after Nan left. The company had moved uptown, from a mercantile district to the center of town; the offices were grander than they had been and secretaries were more numerous. Betty was half mine.

She was a big voluptuous baby, all curves and roundness. She had the sweet, almost confessional smile of a baby and dark velvet eyes. The brows sometimes curved in a seemingly angry frown, but I never saw her angry. She giggled often with a little gurgle. She often shook her head as if physically clearing her mind, and her taffy hair swirled.

She came from Long Island. Her family was well-off. She had been to Bryn Mawr and had just graduated cum laude. I was the first in our office to interview her, and I asked her why she wanted to be a secretary. She said she was interested in publishing. I said that was fine, but there was no surety that this job would lead to anything better. She said she wanted to live in New York. I didn't ask why she couldn't have done so without a job because it was plain, given the facts about her background, that she didn't want, or couldn't get, help from her family.

Later, and not much later, I learned that her father would not help. In those days many parents still felt that unmarried daughters, even sons, ought to live at home, so I thought I understood. But her father had added, "Anyway, you'd never be able to make it on your own." When she told me that, about two weeks after she started work, she said it with a sad shared look, as if I knew her father, knew her difficulties.

Betty did her work perfectly well, was naturally pleasant, got on well with the other secretaries. This last was remarkable because, in the days before secretaries became assistants, most of them college graduates, she was much more one of us, the editors, than one of them. The other girls were a bit sniffy at first, but Betty dressed simply and asked their advice a lot, and they soon saw that she was grateful for their friendship. The editors and bosses all felt that she was like a cousin working for us as a kind of interim lark, unlike the other girls who were doing more or less what they would always be doing, at least until they got married.

She had many boyfriends, and she often went away on weekends. When we chatted, which we frequently did in my office and occasionally did at lunch, she would talk about how she loved being in love. Once I teased her about her weekend activities, and she said, "You're worse than my father." Then she shook her head and the hair swirled and the velvet eyes looked warm and she put her plump hand on mine and said, "No, good grief, you're not."

Then, suddenly, she was out of the office for four days. The girl with whom she was most friendly telephoned her at home on the afternoon of the first day she didn't appear. There was no answer. Betty telephoned the next day. She said she was ill and was staying with a friend and didn't think she could be back until Monday. She apologized and hoped we would forgive her. She sounded odd, as if she were very tired. Or had been crying.

Betty was at her desk when I arrived on Monday. She was pale. She was so contrite, she looked so defenseless yet so ready for the worst, that no one wanted to do anything about the absence. It had been a virus, she said.

A few days later she and I worked late together. When we finished, it was dark outside and the office felt intimate. I said that the next time she got sick she ought to let me know, at once. I said that I had been worried until I heard from her, which was true, and that I had thought of trying to get in touch with her family or even calling the police to open her apartment.

Her brown eyes overflowed. She reached across the desk and grasped my hand. "I really love you," she said. She giggled. "Is it OK to say that?"

It was OK.

After a moment she said, "Can I tell you something? Between us?" I nodded. "I wasn't sick. Not that way, I was up at Crystal Lake." A psychiatric hospital and rest home in Connecticut, famous, expensive. "They know me. I've been there before. A little thing with a lot of pills, as they say." She giggled again. "I can drop in any time I like. Standing invitation. So I just went there."

Nan passed through my mind, faster than she ever

moved in reality. I asked Betty, since she had said that much, whether she wanted to say more. What had happened? Why had she gone to Crystal Lake?

She shrugged. "The usual. I saw my father the Saturday before." Again she said it as if I understood. I must have looked baffled. She went on. "Oh, you know, he told me I'd never amount to anything. Just because I had this nothing little job, I thought I was such a hotshot, but I'd never be anything. Besides, I'm no good. I'm rotten, to say the least. You know, the usual." She shook her head, clearing her mind. "The only thing he'll pay for is Crystal Lake. And my shrink. And he's the reason I need them both." She got up. "This is terrible. Why should you have to listen to all this hooha?"

I asked her to sit down, and asked her whether she had any brothers or sisters. "A brother. Older. He's at Penn Med. My father thinks he's the greatest thing since sliced bread. I like Davey myself, I'm crazy about him in fact, but he can do anything he wants and get away with it. With me, it's," she ducked her head, "different." She shrugged. "Oh, phooey." But the dismissal didn't work for her. Her eyes came back to mine.

I felt cold. I didn't want to hear any more, and I wanted to know everything. A father whose behavior sent his daughter to a mental hospital. And who knew it because he paid the bills — had agreed in advance to pay them. I wanted to know what was in the shadows, and I also wanted to keep out of them. I said, "I wish there was something I could do. More than say I wish there was something I could do."

She grabbed my hand again. "Darling, you're wonderful to me." She said "darling" with a family face. "You're all wonderful to me here. I feel better in this office than any place else in the world." Her chin went down into her neck. "You wouldn't fire me, would you, after what I've told you? I can do the job."

Yes, she could do the job. No, I wasn't going to fire her.

But I did, in time. At least I told my own boss that we had to get someone dependable, and he fired her. He felt wretched about it, as did everyone else. It was not possible to dislike Betty. By that time everyone knew that she had episodes, though not many knew about the father. Everyone knew that she had to be replaced.

All that had happened, really, was that the film had speeded up. The absences happened more frequently. I guessed, and she acknowledged with a duck of her head, that troubles with the father had increased.

Her life with boyfriends had speeded up, too. There were more of them, and when she talked about them, the stories all seemed somewhat frenzied. It was easy to see that she needed the reassurance that male attention gave her; it was harder to see how she — irresistible, soft, endearing — could need it so badly.

Then, after three absences in four months, she was out for ten days. Her girlfriend called Crystal Lake after the second day to confirm that she was there. Betty couldn't come to the phone. On the fifth day I went into my boss's office. He knew what I had to say from the look on my face.

When she came back, he called her in and told her. She came straight from his office to mine, her eyes moist, her face full in its frank baby smile. She spoke before I could. "Darling, don't feel bad." She put her arms around me; she smelled fresh. "Don't feel bad. You had to do it. I know that. I'll be all right. I need to take a rest, anyway." She giggled. "That sounds crazy, doesn't it?" She giggled at that, too, then she said, "My father will pay for it, I guess."

She went somewhere in the Caribbean for a week. She sent me a card. A few weeks later she called me at the office and said she had to see me. She sounded strained. She was at a coffee shop down the street. I was in the middle of something, but I put it aside and went down.

She was sitting in a booth, wearing chic clothes and a number of bracelets. She looked brown and happy. She waved and jangled. She kissed me and began to chatter, no trace of the strain that I had heard on the phone only a few minutes before.

We had coffee and she went on, almost without stopping, about the Caribbean island and the parties there. "I mean," she said giggling, "practically gang bangs." She had never said anything so explicit before. And she said she had just come back from a weekend party with a couple of men.

Now, oddly, I felt less frightened for her. I felt myself looking at her, drawing back. The more she chattered and giggled and jangled the bracelets, the more separated I felt. She hadn't really needed to see me, of course. I thought of the work I had interrupted more than I thought of her. She had just wanted to talk: so I didn't ask why she had phoned.

I changed the subject, trying to make the change sound parenthetical. "By the way, I meant to ask you. Your doctor. You once told me you were seeing a doctor. Is that still on?"

"You mean my shrink? Oh, sure. When I get up early enough. Why shouldn't I go? My father is paying for it. Listen, darling, do you know Jack LaBella?" A band leader. I didn't know him. "I met him last night. *Wild.*"

I got away as soon as I could manage it. I embraced her and smiled as she smiled and felt her warm and close and far away. I went upstairs and got back into the work as hard as I could, I pulled it around me for snugness.

One afternoon the following week she called again from the coffee shop. I begged off, saying I was late for a meeting "inside."

"Oh." A child's gasp. Then she poured. "Darling, of course, of course."

A month later she telephoned me at home, after midnight. Laura answered. She had heard about Betty, she had met her and she liked her. She was as friendly as possible at that hour. "It's for you," she said after a moment. "Betty."

Betty said, "Darling, I'm sorry I disturbed your wife. I'm sorry. And you." She began to cry. "Darling, could you please come for me?"

"What?" I was in bed, I had been asleep. "What's the trouble? Where are you?"

Crying, she said, "I'm at a party. It's terrible." Now I heard the noise behind her, the music and babble. She began to cry really badly. "It's terrible. I want to go home. I can't do it alone."

"Isn't there someone there who can take you? Whoever brought you."

"*No.* Nobody. I don't *like* anyone here. Darling, I need you to take me. Please. I need to go home. *Please.*"

What shocked me most was not her condition but my response. I wanted to slither away over the phone, to slide out of her life. I felt as if an octopus with bracelets were reaching for me. Maybe she really needed help, maybe not, but if I let her call me out of my home at this hour, just once, I might as well cut my throat. She would call again. And again. She would devour me.

I don't remember how, but I managed to persuade her to ask someone at the party to put her in a taxi. I forgave her, as she pleaded with me to do, for calling so late.

Next day I thought of telephoning to find out how she was, but I didn't dare.

A couple of weeks later she telephoned again at home, about two in the morning. This time I answered. She was bright and gurgly. "Hi, darling," she said. "Guess where I am. Florida. Miami. Moon over Miami. Wild, ha? I know you worry about me, so I wanted to let you know where I am. I came down yesterday with some wild guys. Guess what we're doing now. We're sitting by this fabulous pool in the moonlight. Skinny-dipping." She giggled. "It's wild. I love it. I just wanted to talk to you, darling."

I wasn't angry. I thought it was horrible enough to feel as distant as I did without being angry, too.

I saw her once more, I heard from the girlfriend in the office that she had gone back to Crystal Lake again, and a month or so after that, Betty came into the office one afternoon. She was dressed exquisitely, her hair had just been done, she was wearing a gorgeous fox stole. Her face had changed. Now the smile seemed fixed. The velvet eyes had burning pinholes in their centers.

She moved from desk to desk around the office, from cubicle to cubicle, talking incessantly. I wanted to hide, but my room was at the end. I couldn't possibly get out, get past her, without being seen.

She reached me. "Darling." She swept in and hugged me as if I were sick and she were visiting my ward. She chattered on about how busy she was these days having fun, and I tried to make replies that fitted in the spaces that she left.

She took my arm. "Walk me to the elevator, darling. You're the one I love most around here, anyway." We walked out through the large room to the corridor. "I've got to hurry," she said. "I've got to pick up the result of my Aschheim-Zondek." The pregnancy test. "My *latest* Aschheim-Zondek."

At the elevator I said something about the fur stole. "Like it?" she said. "A present. Not from a man, for a change. I got it for myself." Her face changed. "My father paid." I had never seen her face like that. Two expressions combined: fright and vindictiveness. Real fright, yet somehow weary. And the knife look of a vindictive woman.

I went back to my office feeling dizzy. Something had hit me, had spun me around. I couldn't stop spinning.

Her father wanted her. *Wanted* her. He was trying to kill her to protect himself.

If that was true — I didn't know, but it fit what I saw — he got his wish. She was back in Crystal Lake a few weeks later. A few days later I heard from her friend in the office that she was dead. At Crystal Lake. The girl didn't know how Betty had done it, they wouldn't say.

Everyone in the office felt struck. We had dreaded it in advance, but it hurt just the same. I felt something else, too. I was relieved. No more calls. No more octopus.

I never met the father, never saw a picture of him, nothing. I don't often think of Betty, I got fairly well rid of her. But when I do think of her, I think of him, too.

3

Jean Avery was on the bus that we were taking upstate for a weekend. We hadn't seen her in about ten years. She whooped when she saw us, spread her hands, jumped up and kissed us both. Short brown hair, darting eyes, high cheekbones, husky voice, vigor and firmness — all familiar at once. She was now in her middle forties, but even close she looked twenty-five, like a young woman who had lately been a college girl.

She was going up to Harmony, she said as we settled into seats, which was not far from where we were headed. She was going to sell her house. We remembered the house well. We had stayed there several times with her and Tom. Now, as we knew, Tom was dead: his bad heart had taken him off several years before. She was living in Chicago, had decided to stay there, so she was selling the house.

"Say! Why don't *you* two buy it?" she said, grabbing Laura's arm next to her and reaching across Laura, across the aisle, to me. "You always loved it. Why don't you buy it? There's an offer, but it's not final. You could still have it."

I said we wished we could buy it, which was almost true. It was a small early-eighteenth-century Dutch farmhouse, stone walls two feet thick, set on a hillside shelf looking south over a wide valley. I saw it now with memories of Jean gardening decisively in shorts, a cigarette in the corner of her mouth. But in any case I wouldn't have wanted a house redolent of Tom.

We talked along for the two hours until the town where we were all getting off. The longer we rode, the more I liked her and remembered how much I had always liked her and disliked the dead Tom for having shunted us apart. He had been a writer, not a bad manufacturer of sentimental stories. I had published a novel of his, at the firm where I worked after the one where I had known Nan and Betty. But Tom and I had known each other for some years before that. He was tall, slightly portly, bald with a fringe of curly gray hair, and had a mouth like a woodchuck's. He was smooth and smoothly overbearing. If you had rescued him from drowning, he would have complimented you on your swimming while you were doing it. He had the wide thin knowledge of the hack writer. He was usually right on trivial points of factual dispute. He had a lot of skills: carpentry, baking, automobile repair, radio mechanics. He was even a good marksman. Once he took a .22 rifle out of my hands as we were sitting on a porch and carelessly killed a rabbit thirty yards away. I would have missed. I wasn't competing with him in anything — I couldn't do at all most of the things he was good at, so there wasn't any competition — but he always acted as if I were trying to equal him and could use his encouragement. And he was dirty-minded. His work went bumpily, and his frustrations about it, his poor health, his jealousy about his attractive wife—twenty-five years younger — all found an outlet in aggressive, sleazy raunchiness. It was worst when you were his guest and he knew that you were captive.

I liked people who nipped at me less, who were less hungry for parlor victories. My own frustrations were at least up to the average, but I wanted to spend time with people who didn't need to prove themselves so continually or to avenge themselves pettily on the world in the person of myself. Laura agreed. So, in time, we gave up seeing Jean, in order to avoid seeing Tom. When we read that he had died, we didn't know where she was, and anyway it would have seemed odd to look her up as if we had been waiting for his death to clear the track.

Still, Tom was not an ordinary man. And the story of his marriage to Jean, all true, was like a fantasy.

We told the story to the M.s that afternoon, the friends
with whom we were spending the weekend. When we had
parted from Jean at the bus stop, we said we would ask
the M.s, whom she didn't know, whether it was possible to
invite her for dinner. Jean said she'd love it: she was staying in a motel, her car was in a garage up here. She would
love to drive over and spend the evening with us. The M.s
of course invited her, and before she arrived, we told
them about her and Tom.

He, after a knockabout career on magazines and newspapers and in free-lancing, had become a successful radio
writer in the 1940s, doing a weekly homiletic editorial for
a program sponsored by a huge corporation. He met a
beautiful woman named Claire, about forty, whom he
married. After their marriage he discovered that she had
previously been married three times instead of the once
she had told him about, which was not in itself important
but which made him uneasy. Soon afterward he discovered that she was a pathological liar and otherwise pathological as well — she went on binges of alcoholism and violence. He told frightful stories of public embarrassments,
of bottles flung, of fights in which he had to wrench
knives out of her hand, of her disappearances for four or
five days at a time. She was a devil, he said. But before
and after and sometimes even during these outbursts, she
was diabolically seductive. And when she was calm, when
she really worked at it, she could enslave him as abjectly as
at the very beginning before he knew what was under it
all. He felt that he was married to an inescapable maniac.

One day when he was alone in their Manhattan apartment, the doorbell rang. There stood a sixteen-year-old
girl in an orphanage uniform, with a suitcase. It was Jean.
She was Claire's daughter. All this time she had been in

an asylum in the Bronx, a Dickensian horror chamber as it turned out, half an hour away by subway. Jean was illegitimate, and Claire had simply left her at the orphanage almost sixteen years before, had promised to return for her soon, and had never done so. Now the orphanage could no longer keep her. Jean, with her quick wiry intelligence, had picked up a few clues and had tracked her mother down.

When Claire came home, she was unperturbed. She said she thought she had told Tom about the child. She hadn't wanted a baby around, but a sixteen-year-old would be all right.

Jean had been to public school but knew practically nothing. She didn't even have passable table manners. Tom taught her how to use a knife and fork conventionally, he gave her books and pictures and records, he took her to concerts and jazz sessions and museums. It was soon clear to him that she had an exceptionally good mind. He coached her for college entrance exams, they sat up nights together when Claire was out or sleeping it off. In a couple of years Jean took the exams and passed, well. Tom helped her with her college work.

The inevitable happened, it had happened long before they spoke of it. They were in love.

Claire was getting madder by the month, but in intensity, not at length, always within the confines of binges. The rest of the time she was socially maneuvering and fiendishly entwining. Her increased violence made Tom even more anxious to leave her, and the fact that, when sane, she could cajole her way through the world, soothed his conscience about leaving. Besides, there was now no question that Jean and he had to be together. Claire, blinded either by madness or by her ego when not mad,

184

suspected nothing. As soon as Jean graduated from college, Tom told Claire that they were leaving. He made sure that Jean was out of the house when he broke the news.

There was a storm. Tom was ready. Claire chased him down the hall to the elevator, screaming and clawing. He had to throw her out of the elevator and shut the door.

He discovered that a divorce was unnecessary. When he took steps to file, his lawyer learned that Claire had never actually divorced her previous husband, so her marriage to Tom was bigamous and null. Tom married Jean and bought the house in Harmony. Claire made occasional violent appearances in Manhattan or Harmony — once at midnight in the country with a hatchet — but she soon wound herself around another man. She died about ten years afterward. Tom visited her on what turned out to be her alcoholic deathbed, and he said that she was still so seductive that he had to get away fast.

The marriage with Jean was a Freudian ideal, a figurative father-and-daughter marriage. (Betty Berger didn't even seem a shadow of this when I first heard the story, the matters were so different.) Tom was not well when they married, which Jean knew: he always said that Claire had given him his bad heart. He had to give up radio work. He concentrated on short stories for slick magazines, still a possible way to make a good living in those days and he could do it when and where he liked. He had sporadic success: they could live by what he made if they could deal with interludes of worry. One of his stories was sold to Hollywood. They gave up their Manhattan apartment and moved to Harmony. In the cold months they went south for his health — in those days before Castro, to Cuba.

In the winter of 1954 we spent two weeks with them, as paying guests, in the bungalow they had rented in Varadero. It was a lush, luxuriating holiday, lovely except for Tom, or Tom some of the time. Jean, barefoot and brown, made Cuban coffee, boiled stone crabs in seawater, took us to buy the best macaroons in the world. She was learning Spanish and called Tom Tomás. She was the pet of all the shopkeepers in the pretty town. She taught me Cuban dances, and Tom urged me to dance with her as if to prove his self-confidence. Afterward he would make seamy remarks about her body — he didn't dance much—and would ask whether I agreed, while Jean blushed under her brown and said, "Tomás! Por favor!"

I knew all that he had done for her, I knew he was more complex than I was letting him be in my mind, I knew it was ridiculous of me to resent Tom for Jean's sake because she adored him. It was entirely on my own that I didn't like him, because of the smarmy nagging and the sly discomfiting. Laura didn't mind him as much, but she knew how he was affecting me and she didn't care enough about him to argue strongly. After Cuba we saw Tom and Jean a few scattered times over a few years, then we didn't return an invitation. Time went on, and we simply hadn't seen them, didn't see them.

Tom put out another novel a few years after I left publishing. It failed quite badly and, away from the man, I could feel sorry for him. I read the book and could see in it how anxious he was for success. A year or so later we read his obituary.

4

Jean zoomed up to the M.s' house in the little red convertible that I remembered, then zoomed into the house. She shook hands firmly and swiftly, she smiled her burst of a smile, her body squirmed with energy under her trim cotton dress. I could see the M.s trying to reconcile this radiance, this unmediated self, with the story we had just told them.

After dinner, which Jean devoured, smacking her lips over the good wine — she loved wine and she had learned something about it from Tom — we lounged around the fireplace in the living room, feeling knit. But Jean didn't lounge: she sat, as always, at ease but with her feet gathered under her as if ready to spring, a lighted cigarette in one hand, a pack of cigarettes and a lighter in the other. We talked about the Caribbean. She and Tom had stopped going to Cuba when the government changed. Laura and I were thinking of going to the Caribbean for a week or so the following spring — this was summer — and Jean told us about Martinique. She and Tom had gone there for several winters and had loved it. "It's for me. It's my island," she said. She gave us the name of a small hotel in a cove and told us about the owner.

"In fact," she said, "we flew from there to Florida when Tom had his last attack. That's where he died — in Florida."

I said, "I hope it was quick."

"It wasn't." Her face went bronze. "It wasn't. It was bad.

He kept asking, 'Why can't I die, why can't I die?' "

I felt something like guilt, as if his dying might have been easier if we hadn't stopped seeing him.

Jean made herself brighten. "Anyway, afterward I picked up and went to Chicago."

"Why Chicago?" I asked.

"Well, I didn't want to come back and live all alone up here. Especially in the same house. Even if I could get some kind of job here. And we had some good friends in Chicago — Sid and Mimi Ginsberg. Did you ever meet them?"

"I don't think so."

"Well, they said I had to come and stay with them, they were just wonderful to me, and I did that for a while, and I got a job for a while, and I was in the nuthouse for a while." All in one sentence.

"What? What happened?" I asked.

She shrugged. "I tried to commit," she said as if admitting a prank. "One night I was taking a sleeping pill, and I thought, 'Oh, what the hell,' and I just tipped up the bottle and took them all. I was still staying with the Ginsbergs then and they found me."

Laura looked as if she were going to cry. I felt sore, stabbed, and at the same time I thought: The third. The third beautiful girl.

The M.s were hushed. All of us were trying to believe that we had heard right, that this had come from the humming young woman with whom we had just had so much fun, eating fun and joke-making fun, at dinner.

I didn't need to say anything, and was glad of it: I knew she would continue.

"I still don't know why exactly. Anyway, when I recovered, the Ginsbergs took me to Dr. Diener, I still see him three times a week, and he put me in this nuthouse for a while. You ought to see it. The fanciest place I've ever been in anywhere. Swedish modern furniture, paintings in every room, a home away from home. Sid and Mimi call it the Meshugganeh-Hilton." The Yiddish word, in Jean's non-Jewish mouth, was a lighthearted plea to belong: not to Jews, to the world.

She had stayed there two months. Now she had a place of her own, a floor of a brownstone near the lake. She had a job with a photographer, general assistant, handling phone calls, hiring models, lugging equipment. She swam twice a week at a gym — she was a superb swimmer. She worked two nights a week at a settlement house for black children, teaching reading and coaching games. She had decided to stay in Chicago so she had put the Harmony house on the market. She was here now to deal with an offer.

The evening moved along, and the talk moved elsewhere. But Jean's story was like a backdrop in front of which the rest of the talk took place. Then she said it was time to leave. She thanked the M.s with that bursting smile. She hugged Laura. She hugged me.

I told her I was going to Chicago in December for a meeting. Would she like to have dinner? She grabbed my shoulders. "Would I? *Would* I? Do you promise?"

In mid-November I telephoned her, and I could see the smile when she heard me. We made our date. I asked her to book a table for us at any restaurant she liked.

On that night, which was bitter cold, she opened her door with a look that warmed me on the front step. She hugged me and took me in. She talked rapidly, almost breathlessly. She lived on the first floor of her brownstone, and she had a few things I remembered from the

Harmony house. No picture of Tom was visible. She had bought a bottle of Irish whiskey, which she knew I liked, and we had a drink, while she sat opposite me with her feet under her, her cigarette going. She calmed down a little, and we talked and laughed. After a couple of drinks we went to dinner, a quiet good restaurant in another brownstone nearby. I went over the wine list and chose a Musigny. It was a mistake. She drank it as enthusiastically as she could.

The dinner was long and easy. It was the only substantial time we had ever spent alone with each other. We both realized that, without mentioning it, and it gave her a freedom to talk, different from the freedom that she usually had. Partly, I thought, it was childlike excitement about the moment. Partly it was because, like many women, especially beauties, she could talk more freely to a man.

She told me she was busy these days, she liked it, she felt good. Was the doctor helping? "Who knows? I think so. I like seeing him, I like talking to him, but he keeps telling me that I have to help myself. For this, I'm paying him half my salary." She laughed from far inside that warm body. "I'm kidding, of course. He tells me more than that. Anyway, I like talking to him. And anyway it *is* all up to me. Only —"

I waited.

"Only sometimes I'm sitting inside a black shell. You know? Not big. Almost sort of cozy. All the things I do, the job, the settlement house, the people I see, I'm moving around the whole time inside that black shell. Like a nice cozy one-man tank. One-woman."

"Do you tell your doctor?"

"Oh, sure. He says to *use* the tank, until it wears out.

Anyway, it's not there all the time. Like now. Anyway, the hell with it." She held out her glass. "Let's have some more of that delicious wine."

I asked whether she had any social life.

"Some. But it's hard, you know. People don't know what to do with a single woman. They invite you once or twice, try to get someone to match up with you, but it's kind of a drag. They'd rather invite couples."

"But what about men friends? Your own, I mean."

"Oh, a few. Once in a while. Nathan Kahn. I see him once in a while." He was a composer, celebrated, now teaching at the University of Chicago.

"Well, for heaven's sake, that ought to be interesting. How'd you meet him?"

"At somebody's home. Then he called me up. I've seen him a few times. I'm teaching him the guitar. Well, he makes believe I am."

She had learned guitar, at least enough to accompany herself in some songs, in Cuba.

She seemed so unimpressed at knowing this celebrated man that I felt embarrassed at being impressed. I changed the subject. Later we changed wines. Later we were almost the last people left in the restaurant. Suddenly she said, "Stanley, may I ask you something? Why did you stop seeing Tom and me?"

"No special reason, Jean. No special incident or anything like that." I kept talking to cover the hole. "We just drifted apart. You know how these things happen without any real reason, any split, things just carry you one way or another."

She didn't press her question, though she knew I wasn't telling the truth. "Tom was hurt, you know." She had drunk enough to dig a few millimeters beneath even her usual frankness. "He used to talk about it. He didn't know what he had done. He really liked you, Stanley."

I felt irritated. I was sure Tom had said it if she was telling me so, but I thought he had been performing for her. He was shrewd enough to know exactly how he had put me off or at least that he *had* put me off. For Jean, he had been playing the kindly suffering old saint, one of his many roles.

I couldn't think of anything to say. I made a sound — ruminative, I hoped, quasi-repentant.

"I'll tell you something, Stanley," she said bravely. "He wasn't so terribly fond of Laura. I hope you don't mind my saying so. It was you he really liked. He was hurt that you stopped seeing him."

The hell with him, I thought. I felt good now about having dropped him. It crossed my mind to wonder why Jean had told me that about Laura, but the evening was too pleasant to let me wonder long. Besides, I was glad in a way that Jean had told me: it sealed off Tom. I made the thoughtful sound again.

Soon we left the restaurant and walked to her place in the clear cold night. Underneath, I was still a bit upset, I was surprised to discover, at what she had told me, but I didn't show it. It might have done her some damage. I did the opposite of withdrawing. "Jean, I'm going to be passing through Chicago again in February. Changing planes to go some place downstate. On the way back I could stay overnight here and we could have dinner again, if you want to."

She hugged my arm and said she'd love it.

"I'll phone you again a few weeks ahead of time and we'll make a date," I said. "We can go back to the same restaurant if you like. Except no Musigny."

At the door she asked me to come in. I thanked her but said I had an early date in the morning, which was true.

"But I've still got all that Irish," she said.

"It won't spoil. I'll have some more in February."

"Promise?"

I promised. We put our arms around each other, and she kissed me on the mouth. Her body felt electric through both our coats. Her mouth was warm, friendly, womanly.

In New York, in January, by coincidence I met Nathan Kahn. I was in a bookshop when he came in with a lawyer I knew, who introduced us. Kahn was short, white-haired, with a neat white beard, very handsome. He had been divorced four times. His interest in women was well known.

We chatted for a few moments. He was between terms and had come back to New York, his hometown, to see family and friends. I said that we had a friend in common in Chicago, Jean Avery. In a split second his face went through rapid changes. His eyes widened a bit in surprise, the surprise changed to defensiveness, as if I'd accused him of misbehavior, and just as rapidly the defensiveness changed to kindliness, the avuncular kindliness that men with reputations as womanizers adopt to show that they are quite capable of having simple friendships with women. "Oh, yes," he said like a stage uncle, "Jean. She's lovely. A lovely young woman. I'm very fond of Jean." He chuckled. "She's teaching me the guitar."

"Cuban style."

"Cuban style. Or she would if I could see her. Every time I've called in the last month or two, she's been busy."

Whatever his interest, it certainly seemed stronger than the one she had shown in him. Well, I could tease her about it when I saw her.

193

Early in February, on a Friday evening, I telephoned Chicago. Jean didn't answer. I tried again on Saturday morning. No answer. I supposed she was away for the weekend, so I called on Sunday evening. No answer. I called on Monday morning, at eight-thirty Chicago time, assuming that she would have to be up for work. A man answered. I felt like an intruder, but there was no point in hanging up.

"May I speak with Jean Avery, please?"

"Who is this?"

I gave him my name.

"Oh, yes, I've heard of you. Jean talked of you."

"Is she there, please?"

He hesitated a moment. "I'm Dr. Diener."

"Oh, yes." The psychoanalyst. "I've heard of *you*." If he was there, something was wrong. "May I speak with Jean?"

He hesitated another moment. "I'm afraid I have some bad news. Jean has done away with herself."

What a stupid remark, I thought. Did away with herself. What other self is there, I thought, to stand outside herself, to do the doing *to* herself?

I said, "What?"

"She came home on Friday afternoon, apparently, and she was found last night." He sounded solemn but not unhappy, like a funeral director.

She had been lying there the whole weekend. Every time I had called, the phone had been ringing in the room where she was lying. While I was hearing the phone ring, she had been there, not hearing it.

"The police called me," he said. All three of them, I thought, with psychoanalysts. "They've just left," he said.

From newspapers, from television, I had a glimpse of

the police carrying out a stretcher, wrapped. Down those steps where we had hugged.

I thought of the Irish. Still there? Who would get it?

I said some things, routine, knowing that he was being patient with me while I said them. I insisted that he take my address and telephone number in case there was anything I could do, any information I could give. I never heard from him.

I felt a completion, iron but inevitable. I saw her, though I had not seen her, at Tom's door, sixteen, the orphanage dress, the suitcase. All her life, a time bomb in her. Tom had been able to smother it for a while. I thought better of Tom now, but I didn't want that, I wanted Jean to be alive, to have our February dinner, to give me another chance at choosing wine. I heard the steel door of a giant vault, finely milled to fit precisely, swinging into place.

Later that day I thought of Betty, too. They went, they both went, I thought hollowly. I survived. It was just a matter of time, of course, but meanwhile I had survived.

We changed the reservations for our spring vacation. We didn't want to go to Jean's hotel, to Martinique, to her island. We went to Guadeloupe.

Album of London, 1951

1

Lᴏɴᴅᴏɴ, ɪɴ ᴛʜᴇ Jᴜɴᴇ ᴏғ 1951, seemed sacred. I had never been there before, had never been in Europe before, and I arrived with two lights in me. One was the thought of going to the source of English. The other was the thought of seeing the country that had undergone the Blitz, had suffered so much to help win the Hitler war. I had not been in the war: for physical reasons I had been deferred and had done some small volunteer things at home. London was the first place I set foot where the war had actually been. Shakespeare, Dickens, and V bombs. Laura said, as we got off the plane, that I looked tense.

In those days the Atlantic flight was different. After New York there was a fueling stop in Newfoundland. That stop made the flight feel like more of an accomplishment — a running start, a pause to gather up, then a leap. We had wanted to go by the British line, and their plane was like a big boat. We had berths, which were let down like those in Pullman cars, but they were jokes. When your ear touched the pillow, you got the sound of the motors — props, not jets — louder than otherwise.

I wouldn't have slept much, anyway. When I saw, in earliest light, the first rocks off the west coast of Ireland, I felt as if I had put them there, like an architect who sees his plans in proof. Ireland, England, Europe were being made to my specifications as we approached. Everything was what I expected, and was surprising, too.

At the London airport we were met by Reggie Hand, his wife, and their small son. I had come to London on business for Eagle Books, the New York publishing house where I was an editor, and Reggie was the head of the British subsidiary, Allied, that Eagle had lately founded. Reggie was smiles, sparkling rimless eyeglasses, lean cheeks, and vigor. Margaret, his wife, was a younger version of the queen, solid and sedate and dewy. Their boy, Colin, about four, in knee pants and blazer, was curious about us for a moment, then tagged along at his mother's hand, curious elsewhere.

We all had a cup of tea at the airport — they weren't coming to our hotel with us because they lived in Slough, in the other direction — and I tried to act as if I were still on earth. But the cheap table and chairs, the seedy waiter, the pallid tea, the crumbly toast all seemed to me unearthly, summoned from somewhere to sustain an illusion. The Hands asked about our flight, Reggie told me that a desk had been put aside for me at the office, that his colleagues were eager to meet me next morning, that appointments had been made as I had suggested, and I kept wanting to ask: "Did you see air raids? Did you hear bombs? How does it feel to be English? To live among these old names?"

Colin played around the table like a locomotive. When Margaret offered him a bit of toast, he said, "Foo-ee poo-ee" and puffed on. Margaret smiled. "Can't say I blame him. It's poor stuff, this. Not proper toast, over coals. I don't suppose you have coal fires in the States?"

Not in New York anyway, said Laura.

"I know," said Margaret, "I've seen it on the films. You have central heating. I'm sure it's lovely, but I don't think I could ever be quite easy without a coal fire."

I couldn't believe I was talking to a contemporary. I couldn't believe, yet, that I was in a place where someone could say that.

Reggie arranged for a porter to handle our bags, then they walked us out to a taxi. We passed a huge W. H. Smith news kiosk and bookstall. In the book section, prominently shown, were some copies of a novel of mine that had recently been published in Britain. It was astonishing. I had already seen copies in New York, it was the third book of mine to be published here, still I couldn't quite realize that there was a whole country entailed in those different-looking books I had received. It was mystical, to walk into a strange country and find myself there.

Laura saw the book and exclaimed.

Reggie smiled and flushed and said, "Yes, we saw it on the way in. Splendid, isn't it? I'd awfully like to take credit for laying it all on, but it was W. H. Smith's idea."

Margaret said, "Isn't it smashing? It's perfectly smashing."

"It *is* nice," I said, wanting to shout.

We were glad that the Hands didn't ride into London with us, it gave us the chance to be quiet if we chose. It gave me the chance to marvel at the taxi itself — the high old car like a top hat on wheels, the sliding door next to the driver as the only way in, the driver himself in a double-breasted suit and necktie and curled-brim felt hat. I knew I was being naive, and I didn't want to waste a moment of it.

The city itself made my eyes moist and my throat dry. It looked so grimy. The buildings looked so low. It all seemed so tired and wide and great. There were still large gaps, still piles of broken stone and brick. It was consecrated ground, especially because of the pathetic shop

windows, the half-hearted billboards, the people busily
threading their lives in and out through the streets, the
kids playing just as if it were an ordinary place. I began to
recognize names on street signs. Hammersmith!

Our hotel was the Rembrandt, opposite the Victoria
and Albert Museum. It was what I wanted it to be,
frumpy and orderly, brown and dim. In the back of the
lobby I saw a group of formally dressed people coming
out of a banquet room, chuckling and murmuring. It was
a wedding party. I learned later that the Rembrandt was a
favorite place for friends' weddings. No one had been
married there himself, but everyone had a friend who
had been married there.

In the elevator, the lift, I told the operator our floor,
and he said, "Ankyou, sir." It was the first time I heard it.

We went to the theater that night. I've forgotten the
play, but I remember the prostitutes in the doorways of
Brewer Street off Piccadilly Circus. They were the first I
had ever seen in a street. In my span one could grow up
in New York without seeing streetwalkers. I began to feel
traveled.

2

Next morning I came out of the hotel, crossed the
street, and took a bus to work, feeling double, native and
Martian. The Allied offices were in a small former em-
bassy off Babbage Square near Wigmore Street. Not all of
it had yet been leased since its diplomatic service. The
ground floor was vacant; the large double doors were

open on a beautiful parquet floor, a pile of rubble in the center, and a great marble fireplace beyond. I walked up the curved stone staircase to the door of Allied and went out of grandeur into plywood partitions.

Reggie Hand hardly gave me a chance to tell my name to the young woman at the front desk, he was out of his cubicle smiling, glasses glinting. He introduced me to the young but dignified Miss Dobbs, who was to help me as needed. Then I met Simon Verger, the one editor, a young man who was short but who managed to seem lanky, who seemed to present his shoulder bones in friendship. Then I met Bob Thorley, the sales manager, tall and sandy-moustached, who had a little limp. The war, I thought at once. Verger gave me reserved owlish warmth, Thorley spoke quietly, as if he and I were resuming, cordially. I was one of the first from their New York owner's office to visit them and I knew that this was at least part of the reason for the welcome, but I didn't care, I was glad of it. I was shown to a desk in a corner that was to be mine for my stay. There were some letters for me and a typewritten list of appointments.

Eagle and Allied were both paperbound firms, and the object of my trip was to find British books, hardcover, that had not been committed for paperbound reprinting, salable books that had escaped the eyes of previous American scouts, recently or not. If I found anything especially good, Eagle would then "plant" it with an American hardcover publisher as prelude to reprinting it in America and, through Allied, in Britain. My job was tough. Eagle had chosen me for it, they said, because I had as good a chance as anyone of succeeding and because they wouldn't care if I didn't find anything: the trip would be useful — experience for me, attention for Allied.

For the next two weeks I bustled around the center of London in taxis, visiting publishers. That was the first part of the trip. Then Laura and I were to go off on a holiday, elsewhere in England and in France. Then would come Part Two of the business trip, another week in London when I would revisit the publishers I had seen. They would have had time to comb their lists, I would have had time to read some of the books I had already been given.

Most of what I remember of London in 1951 was engraved in offices or at business lunches.

The head of a publishing house couldn't close the door of his office squarely. "Been like that ever since the buzz bombs," he said.

A literary agent, a woman, was lunching with me in a restaurant. She was busily discussing contracts. Behind us, a waiter dropped a glass. She went white. She stammered. Then she smiled quickly and said, "Sorry. Whenever I hear breaking glass. Sorry."

The same woman spoke about troubles with the mail from America during the war. "But there was something very strange. The only thing that always came through, or so it seemed, almost without fail, was the *New Yorker*. I never understood it. It was incredible. Nothing else would arrive for weeks, but the *New Yorker* was unfailing. Incredible."

The sorriest publisher I visited, a pompous little scrubber who dealt in eighth-rate novels and inspirational texts, had a Victorian office near Paddington Station. A frightened old serf in a knee-length gray office coat showed me up a steep flight of wooden stairs to a stuffy room where this wing-collared tyrant waited, beetle-browed. The serf bowed three times as he showed me in, the boss literally waved him out. Then in his wing collar and morning coat, the head of this house tried to sell me *Flames of Araby* and *Clean Chaps Are Happy Chaps.*

Another man, the middle-aged inheritor of a high publishing name, received me in his private office, which had once been the drawing room of this town house where his firm was located. He wore a shabby Savile Row suit, a wrinkled white shirt, a soiled collar, a stained bow tie. His courtesy was kingly. I asked if his firm had been in these quarters for a long time. It was clearly a question that pleased him, especially from Americans. He said that this was the room in which his great-great-grandfather had introduced Byron to Scott. He seemed to form his words off in a past almost as remote as that meeting: they came gently toward me down a long vista, taking fine porcelain shapes as they neared. We chatted. A tinkle sounded outside the double doors. "Ah," he said, "I hear the approach of tea." He turned to me with a roguish smile. "Of course, I know you Americans prefer Coco-colo."

And there was another publisher in a former drawing room, a long rectangle. It was a dank June day: my marrow was chilled. In this long room there was a fireplace at the other end from the desk, and in it a small electric heater. I tried hard not to complain about the cold, but the boy on the bicycle met the tree. As I felt myself about to shiver, I asked whether that heater was on. "Yes," said the publisher, commiserating, "beastly hot, isn't it?" He got up and threw wide the window behind him.

Through those two weeks, doing business and being wide-eyed at the same time, I was busy from Paddington to Bloomsbury, scurrying by comfortable taxi, walking in the narrow streets and across the many squares, priding myself on how quickly I learned short cuts and landmarks. I smoked an English pipe, carried a pocket box of wooden English matches, and drank a good deal more than I was used to, particularly beer at odd hours. I felt engaged in an initiation rite. The doing of business in this city was a secret blessing, a way to get inside on true pretenses. How proud I was that I didn't have time to visit the Tower or see the changing of the guard at Buckingham Palace. Laura, while I was busy, was being taken to Wimbledon tennis by my own English publisher or to tea at the House of Commons or to people's homes, close or distant, getting another London outside the tours. I, in a dream that I tried to keep hardheaded, was swimming through the crammed days, up and down wide stairs and narrow stairs or in lifts that were always tiny, in grand rooms and plyboard excuses, drinking and eating and drinking. For most of my life I had wanted to be here, but I had never imagined such a plunge.

What the photographs and films and books had not prepared me for were the smells and sounds. The smells I remember are of pubs, of English cigarettes, the London underground, London newsprint. The most significant sound, the sound that still brings all after it, was the English telephone. Double ring. Pause. Double ring. I had heard it in films, of course, but until it happened at my elbow, until I myself picked up a phone that rang this way, I didn't realize how it fit the country. Double the American ring yet more casual.

Everything I saw and heard and smelled, no matter how remote or trifling, seemed connected to a musty heroism, a sense of uncomplaint, of having come through an agony and not yet realizing that they were too spent to stand.

More than one man said of another man that he had "a good war record," something I had never heard in New

York. Heads of firms wore unmatched suit jackets and trousers. Reggie Hand had only one suit. At theaters I saw airy women in faded dresses with cardigans over them. I had brought a box of cigars with me from New York, but I couldn't smoke them in public: people looked at me as if they knew I was smoking the price of a meal. The pipe I bought in Jermyn Street seemed average size to me, but Simon Verger, whose pipe had a bowl half the size, teased me. "That's an export pipe," he said. "None of us could afford to fill it." Several times when I had to leave a taxi in a hurry and couldn't figure the tip, I held out my hand with some change in it and asked the driver to take the tip. Always he liked the compliment and picked carefully. So many of the buildings were smoke-blackened, so many wooden hoardings were around bomb sites still being cleared, so many doors were use-darkened around the doorknobs, so many light-switches were gray. The commissionaires at the theaters, the doormen, wore their war decorations on their theater uniforms. Brown Windsor soup became a name in my life, on the official price-fixed menus that still prevailed in pubs and restaurants. I became fond of the smaller-size English typing paper.

I got an image of London as huge, round, oaken, worn: a lovely old tub of a town.

3

But I got another London as well. The imagined city, imagined and at the same time true, the hero city that even in its diversity seemed bound by courtesies of shared travail, showed other sides. I was lucky, in the long run anyway, to see them, too.

We met an actress named Ursula Banks, who was playing a small part — which was all she ever played — in a successful comedy. She was a black-haired woman in her thirties, of great friendliness and voice and thirst and sexual appetite. The last was gossip, the rest apparent. Ursula had a small mews flat, little money, and less care. One of the ways she got drinks and men was to invite friends to give parties at her flat. They would provide the drink, and she would choose a man at the party whom she asked, discreetly, to remain after the others had gone.

"Darling," she said on the phone one day, "this Sunday. Many publishing chaps. Five o'clock or so. You both must come."

I said we'd love to.

"Oh, and darling," she said, "you will produce drink, won't you? Much drink. You don't mind?"

In those days the word "American" was always preceded in England by the word "rich," silent or spoken. I said yes of course.

Laura found somewhere three bottles of American gin. English gin at that time was about half as strong. We didn't know this.

It was a perfect mews, with an ornate arch over the entrance, the kind of elegant useless structure that helps to define the past. Ursula's house was the sootiest on her side. Noise bulged from her two open windows as we trod the cobbles toward her blue door.

The crowd, the small living room, seemed to embrace us. We delivered our bottles, and Ursula said, "Darlings, how blesséd. We're parched." She gestured with her prematurely veined hand at four or five empties on a sideboard. Laura undertook to mix drinks as I, recognizing a few faces in the mob, slipped into it.

Ursula introduced me to a neat man in a dark suit, a white shirt and stiff collar, with a silver tie in a precise knot. His clothes were unusual because most of the others were less well dressed, the men in worn sports jackets, the women in rummage-sale things. "You *must* meet this man," Ursula said to me loudly, in front of him. "Tony has just started his own publishing. Marvelous. Gorgeous books." His name was Tony Lassiter. We shook hands more or less. She left us.

"Yes," he said languidly, as if I were reporting to him. His voice cut through the babble. He was in his thirties. He looked carved of ivory. "Yes, I know. You're Ursula's American. I have been told. In publishing, hmm?"

By now I was used to anti-American feeling. It wasn't uncommon, but it was restrained, often put jokingly. I wrote it off as natural in people who had endured so much more than their allies, were still enduring more. I hadn't yet had it thrust at me.

Yes, I said.

"Any particular house?"

Quite particular. Two, in fact. The British one was Allied.

"Mm," he said, as if he had known and had been testing my truthfulness. "Paperbounds, I believe. A person named Hand."

He rose from the back of the sofa on which he had been sitting and moved off.

I turned to others, then to others, all pleasant, engaging, stimulating. Then something odd happened. The party began to melt. People didn't leave, in fact a few

207

more arrived, but all of them seemed to dissolve slightly, like snow men and women under a rising sun. I soon found the reason. They were drinking martinis. They were used to gin-and-French, as they called it, mixed half and half. With English gin. Laura was making martinis, three to one, with American gin. The room became like a scene in a film where the focus shimmers to suggest a dream.

Ursula, a veteran drinker, was only tiddly. "Divine drinks, darling," she said as we met somewhere in the room. "You and Laura must do all my parties. How did you and Tony get on?"

I told her, briefly.

She waved her old woman's hand at the end of her young arm. "Piffle. Don't be put off. He's a duke's nephew, and he can't forget it."

I could, I said.

"But he does publish gorgeous things." She told me the name of his house, and I vaguely recalled a smartly printed brochure.

A man took Ursula away. I wound through the dissolving room, steady because I wasn't drinking gin. Inevitably I encountered Lassiter, again on the back of the sofa, one of the few other steady figures. He was sipping red wine, swinging one leg.

"Ah, yes," he said, "the vendor. Small room here. Bound to meet again. Well! Vended anything since last we met?"

I told him he was mistaken: rich Americans didn't vend, they bought.

"Of course," he purred. "Silly of me. Land of steaks and butter, yes? Well! Buying hot properties, are you?" He relished the Yankee phrase.

None hot enough so far, I said. The available British books were tepid.

"Poor old Brits. Can't write any more, alas. Or perhaps," he said, "it's the offers that are tepid?"

Not especially, I said. For instance, if he had any books we could use, we might make him a non-tepid offer. For American and British paperbound rights.

He sipped his wine, amused. "And what would that be?"

Two hundred pounds advance, I said. I knew that, though this was less than the equivalent of what Eagle often paid in New York, it was about four times the going advance in London at the time.

When I spoke the words "two hundred pounds," a terrible thing happened. His face changed, not slowly. The words did to him what the gin had done to the others: he melted. He knew he was changing, he knew he was losing himself, he knew he couldn't help it. He flushed in the knowledge.

I hated it. I had mentioned the money to see the effect, and I hated it. I liked him better as the Yank-hating duke's nephew. That was his proper role in my experience of London, not this.

After a moment, he managed words. "We might meet," he said.

I said it was possible.

"Perhaps lunch," he said further. "At my club. Might amuse you."

I said it was possible. He said he would ring.

I suspected that he was the man Ursula had tapped to remain after the party. Privately I hoped he would regain himself.

That night I looked over his brochure and saw that

there was nothing in it of use to us. All very English, gardens and horses and minor military biography.

At least he never telephoned. I was grateful for that. At least he recovered his dislike. But that minute amid the drunks was terrible.

4

Then there was Bob Thorley. Quietly chummy Bob, the sales manager of Allied, who took me under his social wing. It was business-world social, nothing like the duke's nephew, it was private restaurants without price-fixed menus and drinking clubs that weren't obliged to heed the legal closing hours. I had been ready to dislike Bob on sight as fitting the pattern of the New York operator, usually taller than myself, who put his arm around me when introduced and favored me with hearty confidences and side-of-the-mouth jokes. Tall Bob approached the same way, limping a bit, but there was no arm around the shoulder and his talk was keyed low.

Bob said, early in my stay, "Some pals I'd like you to meet," but I met only one. He took me to a private dining club in Arlington Street, luxuriously furnished, and introduced me to a small dapper man about forty, with a fringe of black hair around a gleaming head and a voice overly mellow for his frame. "Ted Constable," said Bob as if the merit of the man were now self-evident. I asked if he was one of the publishing Constables. Ted waved his palm at me. "Nothing to do with them. Not related. See why you ask, though, in this company. No, I'm in the advertising dodge."

They were both members in this place, both were fussed over by the staff. The two lunches I had there with them were by far the best meals I had in London that summer. Our talk was never anything but chat, time out from the day on both sides of it.

Their tone implied that they wished I could join, not just the dining club but London itself. "Should have seen it before the war," said Ted. "Right, Bob?"

"Marvelous," said Bob gravely.

"Bloody marvelous," said Ted. "Best place in the world. No offense," he said to me quickly.

None. New York was in my bones, I said, but I thought London was pretty marvelous right now.

"Not bad," said Ted. "But it's changed. The fine edge. Not quite the same."

"Different," agreed Bob. "Things not as, I don't know, right as they used to be. Used to be able to depend on things more. Depend on people."

"Exactly," said Ted. "Cracked a bit. Not the Blitz. I don't mean the bombs. I mean, well, service and reliability and, oh well," he said to me, "you know, all the sorts of things the bloody silly English like about England."

"Place like this," said Bob, nodding at the room, finishing the whiskey he had been sipping with his chops, "gone off a bit."

I said I had wanted to see London ever since I could read, and I was glad to be here even if it was too late.

"Oh no," said Ted, "don't misunderstand. Still bloody fine. And I'm glad you *are* here. You know, in a curious way, Stan, you don't seem a visitor. I mean, you don't sound English or anything of the sort, but you seem to fit. For a Yank. Right, Bob?"

"Thought so from the first," said Bob.

I was being conned, of course, but I didn't see that it could have any aim other than pleasantness. Besides, I liked the conning.

"Bob, we're old enough to have a lager," said Ted. "Let's have a lager."

"Right you are," said Bob and snapped for a waiter. He knew by now — he acknowledged with a wink — that I wouldn't be drinking more after my one luncheon drink. "Two lagers," he confided to the waiter.

"Ankyou, sir."

As we walked out after lunch, I had the impulse to ask Bob about his limp, but I thought it would be crude. A lot of people I saw in the streets had limps or scars or pinned sleeves or carried canes.

Outside the club Bob and I parted from Ted. "Not the last you'll see of me, I'm afraid," said Ted, holding my upper arm. "We need to knock back a few more together while you're here."

I said I'd enjoy it, although I knew it was true only because seeing him was one more way of knitting into London. The Teds at home were another matter.

As Bob and I got in our taxi, he handed the commissionaire a ten-shilling note. That was an immense tip in 1951. I assumed that it was expense-account money, still it was more than lunch itself in many places.

One afternoon a few days later, Bob and I went together to see a publisher in Mayfair. Afterward Bob said, "We're only just across the road from Ted's quarters. Let's nip over for a quick one."

I was interested to see Ted's office — I wanted to see all I could — so I agreed. Beside the doorway of a town house in this quiet street was a modest brass plate: "Constable Co. Advertising Agents." The foyer was dim and expensive. An attractive receptionist recognized Bob. "Oh, Mr. Thorley. Lovely to see you."

"Hullo, Mavis dear, lovely to see *you*." He introduced me, which didn't much concern her.

She said, "Mr. Constable's on a trunk call. I'll just pop in and make frantic signs."

"Don't disturb him, love."

"Oh, he'll want me to," she said, getting up. She was tall and had extraordinary legs. "It's some tiresome Midlands person. Mr. Constable doesn't even want his account. Won't be a tick." She disappeared.

She reappeared and took us into a large room. It was swathed in curtains and rugs, there were two crushed velvet sofas. No publisher's place had been like this. Perhaps there were world standards for advertising people.

Ted, in a rich brown suit and a creamy white shirt, with his jacket sleeves and his shirt sleeves unbuttoned and rolled up, rose from behind an acre of desk; was glad to see us; called us tramps wandering about the streets in search of free grog; opened a mahogany bar and gave us whiskey in wine glasses. He asked me how I was getting on; I said that what I was getting on best with was London. Bob asked him about a new staff man he had been after, and Ted said he'd had to offer the man the earth but he had got him, had to have first-class help because he was overworked. After some more chat I asked Ted about the pretty woman and child in the leather frame on his desk. "Taken last year," he said. "Married a little Yiddish girl four years ago. That's our boy. Couldn't be happier. You must come and see us, you and your good lady wife. Bags of room in our weekend place. Angmering. On the sea. I think you'd like it."

"And a lot of quite jolly people," said Bob.

I thanked Ted, with all the office sincerity I could muster, but I was afraid that time was pressed. He understood. I enjoyed being invited for an English weekend and not being able to accept.

Bob and I left soon. Mavis tipped a fingertip kiss to him. The narrow, white Mayfair street was flowing with people going home. At the corner a man in a cap with a kerchief round his neck was selling flowers out of a huge basket at his feet. At the far corner was a street organ. The organ grinder had a big moustache and a spangled jacket; a little girl in a spangled skirt held out a tambourine for coins. There must have been street noises, but I didn't hear them, I heard only the street organ. I walked through the low late Mayfair afternoon, with Bob and his limp that came from the war.

5

The limp was from the war but not quite as I imagined. Next morning I was in Simon's office at Allied with him and Reggie. Bob was out on business. Reggie, over Simon's scowling protest, pulled a slim book from Simon's shelf and handed it to me. It was a volume of medieval French poetry that Simon had translated. I was impressed.

"Oh, keeps me out of mischief," said Simon. "Partly."

The note on the back flap mentioned Simon's education and previous translations and said that he had spent four years in the RAF. I said that I never asked English people about their war experience because I assumed that everyone here had been in it, one way or another.

"More or less," said Reggie. "Home guard, if nothing else. Like blind old Hand."

Simon said, "I phrased that stuff on the flap very carefully, to sound dashing. Actually, I was a clerk." Clark.

"Actually he did sensitive translation and interpretation of intelligence," said Reggie.

Simon muttered, "Right, Empire couldn't have muddled through without me."

"What about Bob?" I asked. "That limp of his. I haven't mentioned anything, but I assume it was the war."

Simon said "Ahrr" and Reggie twinkled. "I suppose one could say that," said Reggie. "It *was* an army trunk. A trunk fell on his foot. Full of band instruments. He was an army bandsman. Drummer."

He glanced at Simon: Simon looked back, then looked away. I felt that there was something they wanted to say and had decided not to say it. They knew I knew that. That was what they had told me: that they had decided not to speak.

I finished Part One of the business trip. Laura and I went away for two weeks, then came back to London. The very idea of coming back, of returning to London, was spacious. I almost expected to be recognized by the railway porters.

I began my round of follow-up calls. I had visited about two dozen publishers before the break. While I had been away, a few of them had written to say that they had no books for me. With the others, Miss Dobbs had already made appointments. I was rushed: I had one week to deal with two weeks of preparation.

We were to leave for New York on Saturday morning. On Thursday afternoon, quite late, I went back to the Allied office to pick up some books. Only Simon and

Reggie were there. When I came in, I sensed that they had been waiting for me.

There were some small jokes, but they didn't wait long. "Look," said Reggie, sitting next to my desk, "we must speak to you. There *is* something."

I said I had thought so.

"We know," said Reggie, glancing at the owlish Simon. "Sorry to be so sidewise about it, but it's devilish dicey. It's not a matter of confidence in you. Not that at all. It's just that what we say is hard to prove, and besides it sounds so blasted self-serving."

I asked them not to worry.

"Well, thanks," said Reggie worriedly. "Still —" He paused, then went ahead. "Well, we must speak. Face to face. It's not something we can put in a report. We can only tell it to you and hope that you'll put it in the same way to Sam and Fergus." Top officers of Eagle in New York. "Finally it's our jobs at stake because it's the health of the whole blasted company here that's at stake."

My mind raced ahead to guess, but I made it come back to listen.

It was Bob Thorley. They had no absolute proof, not yet, but they believed he was making private deals, with the printing and shipping people, skimming off kickbacks, siphoning off money in other ways. He had been an assistant sales manager with a big publisher after the war and had done pretty well; after he came to Allied he began running around with big-spending types, "wide boys," had left his wife and kid and was "banging about" with women, was betting a good deal, and was generally over his head. He was still good when he worked, but he didn't buckle down to it hard enough. It had been going on for four or five months. Reggie and Simon had been looking forward to my visit because they wanted to speak, not write. Even now it was risky because they could prove almost nothing, but by the time they could prove something, a good deal of damage might have been done.

I thought of London, not the company. I wasn't shocked about Bob, just clarified. Now I knew what all the social plying had been about, with swanky Ted, to lull or even enlist me. But it was London I thought about first. London now was easier to believe.

Goodbye, coziness of the No. 73 red bus, compressing all of us passengers into a temporary club every morning. Goodbye, unflawed warmth of pubs, reassurances of the pearly twilights in the little streets. The next time I saw London I would be a husband, not a swain.

I said I would relay the message, as given, next Monday in New York.

Bob may have suspected that they had talked to me. He may have been saving that last Friday for his clincher with me, to get me in somehow, to lock me to him, then possibly he backed off rather than confirm what I had heard. He went out of town on Friday. But he sent Laura a going-away present, a pretty little enameled trinket box.

6

New York looked like a city in the future that, mysteriously, I knew well. On Monday morning I spoke to Sam and Fergus, and ten days later Fergus went to London. A week after he arrived, Bob Thorley resigned. I heard that he went into advertising with Ted Constable. None of that was surprising. But a month later Reggie Hand resigned, too, to go with another publisher. Simon, the scholar-owl, took over Allied and ran it for years, well.

Soon after we got home, Laura sent a suit to the Hands' little boy, jacket and knee pants. Margaret wrote us a note, saying how much Colin loved it. "And he's absolutely fascinated by the zip on the pants. He keeps undoing it and doing it all the time, in private and elsewhere. Remarks have been made." I had forgotten that zippers were not yet common on English trousers, a wartime restriction. I had noticed buttons in the lavs of restaurants.

Men's rooms are not the key to my London of 1951, but I do sometimes think of those English fly buttons nostalgically. The person from that summer that I think of most often is Bob Thorley. Now he seems like one kind of war casualty, not the drummer's limp but as if he couldn't resist small luxuries, small greeds after a long thin time.

I never heard why Reggie left Allied. Perhaps too much pride to profit by Bob's troubles after he himself had disclosed them, perhaps just a better offer. I never saw any of them again, though occasionally I read Simon's name in a review of a new translation.

Out of the whole trip, all the scurrying and reading, I wasn't able to find one book to recommend to Eagle. As they had promised, no one minded. The trip had been good for Allied, for Eagle, for me, they said.

For me it was true in a way they couldn't know. Five years later when Laura and I went to London on our own and lived there for a bit, it was a different city for me, clearer in fact and in expectation. Still, fact is not everything, sometimes it is not anything. I kept the first London in my head, not for guidance but for thumbing through privately, a city of heroes getting back to tea and umbrellas. Fact had nothing to do with it.

Album of a Western Writer

1

In June of 1954 I needed money badly. I was the editor in chief of a new, small publishing house that had started with a rush two years before. Various mismanagements in the business department had produced a stagnation: the company could possibly survive if no one touched it for three months, when cash might flow again. I was asked to take a three-month leave without pay.

Before I knew about the trouble, Laura and I had rented an old stone farmhouse in Bucks County, Pennsylvania, for the summer. I had intended to commute to the office in New York four days a week. Now there was no need. But I couldn't just sit in the country waiting out my leave; and I couldn't write something with little or far-off possibility of return. I had no real assurance that, after three months, the leave would not be extended or even that the company would weather the lull. Still I didn't want to finish it off, in my life anyway, by looking for another job. I had to make some interim money.

I decided to let the company help me to do it. For the previous two and a half years I had been editing assorted kinds of books. Some of them had been substantial and a few of them are still read, but most of them were company sustenance. Every month, in addition to a general book or two, we had published our category books, as we called them: one science fiction, one thriller, and one Western. A number of these I had worked on myself. One thriller and one Western I had virtually rewritten on weekends because we needed manuscripts and, as a new firm, we were not getting first or even third choices. I knew something of the features of each of these categories, knew approximately the money to be made from them, and decided to choose one.

For science fiction I had no gift. A thriller was possible. I thought a Western might be easier. Besides, I liked the idea of fantasying in Western lingo and open-space action rather than the compression of the city-bound, or at least city-bred, thriller. So I became Terry Kirk.

I needed a pen name because I wrote novels of "my own." Three had been published, in several countries, and a fourth was coming out at the end of that summer. To keep the lines straight, I had to use another name. As a private joke, I chose a minor character in one of my novels to be the author of this Western.

The plot took about a day to devise. I knew that what Western readers wanted was, essentially, one of a limited number of plots all over again, disguised just enough so that they wouldn't feel ashamed of themselves. Sometimes a reader would write the house to say that he had gone halfway through a Western before he realized that he had read it before, and he meant the letter as praise. I knew that the book had to do two things: sound fresh, and celebrate an old ritual, like new music for an ancient ceremony.

I would have finished the plot in half a day but I remembered belatedly a word from an old hand. There had been one real change in Westerns since the war years, he had said, maybe because so many Americans had been overseas and had met European and Asian women. The prewar Western had always had a goody-goody heroine.

Another kind of woman might be prominent in the story — a dance-hall hostess, say — a woman who had been around, understood men, loved the hero, and was true-blue, but the hero never married her. The other woman usually died helping him, and he married the good girl. "Now," said the old hand, "the reader doesn't want that. Don't make the experienced woman *too* bad, then the hero can forgive and forget and marry her, a real woman, instead of a Christmas-tree ornament." It took me the afternoon to revise my plot in the light of that advice. By five o'clock I was ready. Next day I could start *Shootout Canyon*.

I was so eager that night I could hardly sleep. I had never felt like this about any of the money writing I had done. I had done different kinds, and I hadn't always enjoyed the writing itself, but I had always enjoyed finishing it — the neatly stacked pages, crisp and ready to sell, like produce for market. I was young, I had lots of time ahead, it was invigorating to do this other work to support "my own" writing. The money, when I got it, always felt particularly solid, like cash wages in a laborer's hand.

Most of that money writing had in some way been versions of "my own" writing — radio scripts, plays for amateurs, slick magazine stories, one job of Broadway play-doctoring — that trimmed the corners of what I really wanted to write. But the Western had nothing to do with me or "my own" writing. It was like becoming someone else. It made me tingle. When I sat down to begin the next morning, I understood the difference this time. I was acting.

All hack writing is acting, to some extent, even for a writer who never does any other kind of writing. It calls for enthusiasms not wholly your own, maybe not even partly so, which you hope will comfort others, many others. But this time I had taken on a role so far outside myself in experience and values that the act of acting was almost larger than the act of writing. I had never been in the West, I had never been on a horse other than farm horses with backs like lawns, I had lost all my schoolboy fist fights, I had never fired anything but a .22 rifle at rabbits and woodchucks. Still something in me — something that would become clearer — had chosen to do a Western, and when I sat down that morning in the Pennsylvania sunshine, I felt trim and prime. I stepped onto the stage and I was ready.

2

The work went steadily. I saw the book growing as if I were watching a small building going up according to plan. Sixty thousand words. Six parts. Six weeks.

I felt exhilarated. I felt honest. I went to work every morning and did my job. I felt as if I had brought a lunch pail upstairs every day and tucked it under my desk. I was having more pleasure than in any money work I had done before — at one angle, more than in any of "my own" writing where I had to work much harder.

This was because it was double pleasure, double discovery. First, I played Terry Kirk. I didn't walk into the room with bowed legs, I didn't roll cigarettes; I knew successful Western writers who lived in the New York suburbs and carried umbrellas on slightly cloudy days. But I typed as at a workbench, feeling proletarian, and for five or six hours a day I concentrated as hard as I could on narrowing the apertures of my mind, my memory, my ambition, my idea of self-esteem. In that sense I wrote from the inside out. If Stanislavsky could have seen my performance — could *really* have seen it, inside my head — he would not have been displeased.

And there was another element. If I had been playing Terry Kirk on a stage, I would only have had to behave credibly, bashing the keys with intent, typing some memorized passages to fulfill the action. But this performance of Terry Kirk moved out. It intersected planes. In my typewriting as a Western writer, I had actually to type a Western, to write material that would be read as no theater audience would read a stage Terry's work. This was naturalism past the naturalistic: the actor playing a certain kind of novelist had to write a certain kind of novel.

That novel came out of films. The writer himself was a theater creation — I sometimes saw my workroom as a stage set, I even knew which was the missing fourth wall. But the stuff of the writing came from films. The dozens, the hundreds of Westerns that I had seen in my life seemed to have coalesced into a volatile mass somewhere inside me, into which I could dip for flavor and for strength. I didn't have to dip: I can't recall ever having to stop and scratch. Out of that mass of distilled experience, jets bubbled and flowed.

The plot was just a reshuffling of a standard deck of cards that were ready to anyone's hand. But the motion from point to point, the color of the motion, came from sources I hadn't realized that I had stored away: the sunset light on a mesa, a horse picking his steep way between rocks, boot heels locked on the cross bar of a gate while a man watched a branding, the heft of a full holster, the stretch of sleeping on the ground by an open fire. I hadn't realized that my memory, which I had thought consecrated to my own experience in my lifetime, was so much at the service of second-hand experience in the past. I was at least as aware as most people that I had been affected by the culture in which I lived, but I was surprised to find how much of it was in my bloodstream, far beneath daydream. The news was chastening, and it was exciting. I felt linked with the world in new ways, not more closely than before but differently: as if I had discovered that neighbors whom I already liked had been companions in the same wars. The lowest community of privacy, the secrets I shared with all the others that were nevertheless my secrets, made me feel stronger, more ambitious. I felt better qualified as an inhabitant of my society, better qualified to go on to the best work I was capable of, because of all this. Evenings, when I read or listened to music, I felt particularly certified. I planned future projects — "my own" — with a new confidence.

Around this time I began to think about films. I had been going to them avidly all my life. Now I began to think about them.

Inevitably, the characters in *Shootout Canyon* were modeled on film actors or on amalgams of them. The hero, taciturn, not too handsome or perfect; his grizzled, sharp-eyed sidekick who had once been an Indian scout; the limping old swamper who had been lamed by a horse; the villain who didn't drool but who was eaten by several jealousies and by power-hunger; the heroine who had once loved the hero but had been sideswiped into a marriage with the villain (so we knew he was going to be killed) — they were all easy to cast. What amazed me was the tegument, the detail, the smell and thud that welled up easily. None of it came from the Western manuscripts I had edited. I wasn't remembering words: I was remembering fragments of vision and sound.

A theatrical fantasy was being realized through films. I felt like a one-man cultural epiphany.

None of this is to say that *Shootout Canyon* was anything more than a conventional Western. That is exactly the point.

3

A week before I finished the book, I heard that my editorial job was secure again: I would go back to work in mid-September. Laura and I planned a holiday for late August. We would do an auto tour of the deep South, where we had never been, a lazy circle across to the Mississippi, down to New Orleans, across the Gulf country, and up through the Atlantic seaboard.

I finished the manuscript on my schedule and delivered it to my agent who read it promptly. She didn't like the paragraphing on the first page. I retyped the first page and set off for the South.

While we were en route, my fourth novel was published. I had told the publishers of this trip — but not that I had written a Western — and they arranged a few autographing parties for me, in Harrisburg, in Memphis, in New Orleans. Not many people came, not many copies were sold, but I enjoyed the parties. It was nice to be welcomed in places where I was a stranger. Besides, when people complimented me, if they did, on this novel of "my own," I enjoyed thinking of Terry Kirk, of my exultant earthy secret.

After about nine wandering days on the road, we arrived in New Orleans, at a hotel in the French Quarter which was the only place we had booked in advance, the only address I had been able to leave behind in New York. A letter from my agent was waiting, telling me that *Shootout Canyon* had been accepted in three days by the first editor to see it, not my usual publisher. The pseudonym would be respected. The editor was the only person in that office to know — then or later — who Terry Kirk was.

That night we had a good dinner at Galatoire's. Afterward, Laura was tired and wanted to go back to the hotel. I felt restless and went out again. I walked down Bourbon Street and went into a striptease bar that was half-empty. The star was doing her number in a niche behind the bar, a dismal redhead with an odd figure. I was about to finish off my overpriced drink and leave when another stripper came on, brunette, pretty, with a superb figure. I stayed. She was an untalented performer. She went through her sexy routines like a child coached in a school play. Nobody hooted because she was physically perfect.

All the girls mingled with the customers between their turns to promote drinks. After her act the brunette, wearing the costume in which she had begun her number, came up to my tiny booth and asked if I was alone. She had a syrupy Southern accent, not at all New Orleans. I invited her to sit down and have a drink. She ordered one and another for me. Hers was rum and Coke — but without rum, I think; mine was watery whiskey. Five dollars a round.

She had been coached in conversation as in dancing. "Whe' you from?"

New York.

"No foolin'. Ah nevah been theah. What's yo' lahn o' wukk?"

A writer.

"You mean, lahk on a newspaper?"

No, stories. Like in magazines and books.

"No foolin'. What kahnd o' stories?"

Westerns, mostly.

"Westerns? Ah lahk them pretty good. Ah lahk love stories better, though. What's yo' name?"

Kirk. Terry Kirk.

"Well, Ah sho am pleased to meet you, Terry," she said. "Ah'm Velmina. Ah'm jes' about done with this yere drink," she said.

She ordered another round for us, and she asked me about myself. In the air I wrote Terry Kirk's life for the near-naked girl next to me. I forget what I told her, but it took nearly an hour, until she had to go on again, and it cost me another fifteen dollars. It was worth it. It was more acting — backward — to fill the space before the book had been started. I signed a paper cocktail napkin for her. It was the only autographing party Terry Kirk would have.

4

During the next year *Shootout Canyon* was sold to a paperbound reprinter, a Canadian magazine for serialization, a British publisher, a British paperbound reprinter, and a Dutch publisher. With this money and a bit more from other work, Laura and I figured that we could just afford to spend a year in Europe. I resigned my editorial job at the end of 1955. A few days before we sailed, my agent telephoned to say that the film rights of the Western had been sold. It was a small studio, a small sum, but it would make breathing much easier in the European year.

It seemed right that *Shootout Canyon* should feed back into films. I felt like a part of a great natural process: I was sure that there were hundreds of Western novels and films that had come from Western films before them, not so much through plagiarism as through nourishment.

Fourteen months later we were back in New York, and a few months after that, the picture played at Loew's State. We went to the first showing on the first day. The theater was sparsely dotted with sprawling teen-agers — unduly sprawling, I thought. The title had been changed to *Shootout Fury*. The picture had a minor star, who stayed minor and disappeared some five years later. When the credit flashed on the screen "From a novel by Terry Kirk," I was thunderstruck, as if I had idly pressed a button three years before that had just set off an explosion. Throughout the film Laura laughed quietly or shook her head and said "tsk." I was fascinated. Some of the story had been altered, some of the dialogue had been changed, but there it was — my invention — with real rocks, real horses, real punches and pistols. As real, at least, as where they had come from.

Without any such forethought, *Shootout Canyon* became a turning point for me. The hack work dwindled and disappeared. This wasn't an ethical resolve. I began, like every person passing forty, to believe in mortality. I began

228

to be unwilling to take long ways around to where I wanted to go. But I knew that Terry Kirk had stamped my passport, had helped to empower my passage away from him.

About fifteen years later *Shootout Fury* was on late-night television. I watched it. I felt as if I were watching a kind of home movie out of the far past. Invisible, I had the central role.